The Journey

Daddy, you stayed when so many would've left.

Mom, you left far too early, but your love stayed.

Love and miss you both.

Editor – Ronnie D. Wesley

Creative Direction – Lamona Burnett

Foreword

Whenever you're communicating with me, be very basic and give it to me straight, that way we can both walk away happy. Don't use parables, poems, or hints...say what you mean and by all means, mean what you say. Don't assume and please, dot every "I" and cross every last "T." Don't get me wrong, I process things quite well ... most of the time. This is just me being incredibly transparent because there are times when I just don't ... get ... it -- simple as that. One of my "don't get it moments" turned out to be lifechanging.

A friend gave me what she thought was clear direction and, you guessed it, this guy, thought I did everything right only to find out I actually dropped the ball. She called it to my attention, and we went back and forth on what was supposed to be done, what got done, what didn't get done, and how in God's name, I let things go so horribly wrong. The conversation raged for precious minutes that seemed like hours with her becoming increasingly frustrated and me doing the same.

Confused, I asked why she was having such a hard time believing that a simple mistake could have been made, that somewhere along the lines, translation was lost. She turned and shouted, "why is it so hard for you to understand, get things ... communicate?" Not to be outdone, I shot back with, "why is it so hard for you to accept that we just got our wires crossed?" What she said next, changed everything ... "Because communicating is what you do ...

Lynn...YOU ... are a writer..."

She kept talking but after that comment, whatever she said was a blur...nothing more than a bunch of garbled noise. I don't remember a word of it...I got lost in the gift that filled the void where conversation once lived, a door that up until that point had only been cracked, but based on a simple misunderstanding, was now wide open. Oh sure, I scribbled down a couple of things here and there, got a compliment or two ... but this ...

"Lynn...YOU are a writer..."

For years, friends and family members would ask me to compose letters, help out with a project, freshen up a resume, this, or that, but I never thought those requests to be any more than what they were, favors. Little did I know each one was a push, a gift, God beautifully guiding me as only He can toward what He called me to be.

"Lynn...YOU are a writer ..."

I had this job once where I was misemployed as a technical person, developing solutions, and doing all kinds of geeky things. Can I be honest with you? I hated every minute of that job and it showed. One day just to keep me busy (and employed) the Team Leader gave me the task of writing our response to a rather large bid. No problem as I was always a good workplace soldier, willing to do whatever was necessary to get the job done. So, with that, I dutifully went about the business at hand. When I was done, he complimented me saying in all his years, it was the best he had seen. That company eventually downsized and I lost my job but I took that skill (which I now know to be a gift) and built an entire business around it but more out of necessity and survival than a true recognition of a God-given talent.

"Lynn…YOU are a writer …"

I live with my eyes and ears wide open, looking for this, listening for that. From there, I shape and mold those experiences and pass them on to incredibly beautiful people like you with the hopes that in some small way, your life, your journey will become that much more fulfilling.

So, who am I you ask?

A guy who loves and misses his mother … and father …
A proud son …
I'm a younger brother and … a pretty good brother…
A self-described dog lover … who doesn't own a dog, yet …
Long walk lover …
Jazz listener …
I'm the quirky one who likes his food at room temperature…microwaves and stoves are nice, but I'll take mine, especially if it's pizza, at room temperature….
A book lover… if you're looking for me, I'm probably in the bookstore…
I'm a marathon runner …
A mentor…who was once mentored …
Football lover … especially if the team is wearing burnt orange …
A good friend…and on this journey, maybe I can become yours but first, allow me to introduce myself.

My name is Lynn… and … I'm a writer.

Keep Coming by

My parents met in college, on the campus of Kentucky State University. She was a beautiful, polished young girl from Tulsa, Oklahoma, class personified with so much style and grace that she could loan some out and still be head and shoulders above the rest. He was a well-mannered young football player, son of a Methodist preacher, from a tiny town of Thomasville, Georgia.

I like to hear him tell the story of how they first met; it never gets old. He said he was taken by her at first sight and who wouldn't be he always asks? So much so that at the young age of 20, he knew he was sure he had met his wife. Day after day, she'd come into the cafeteria and day after day, he'd admire her from a distance. Each day he got closer and closer until one afternoon, he clumsily (his words, not mine) approached her.

He introduced himself, she introduced herself and from that day forward there was no more admiring from a distance, they became one. Each day they'd meet for lunch and for long walks after class. Now, she had style and grace and she also had trunks and trunks of clothes. Yes, when she came out of her dorm, she looked like she had leapt off the of Vogue. She had shoes, coats, blouses, scarves, earrings, necklaces, watches, perfumes...everything a girl needed, and she was so beautiful; and she was kinda pretty too.

Now, his wardrobe...that was a different story, a challenge in the truest sense of the word. All his clothes were outdated and nowhere near as stylish as hers. Oh, he tried really hard to keep up, switching this shirt out and wearing these pants with a sweater or jacket and sometimes even borrowing from a friend. But as the courtship deepened, he knew when it came to clothes, he was no match for her; not even close.

It wasn't even close, and mom saw how hard that little country boy from Georgia was working. So, one day, as they strolled along campus, she lovingly put his hand in hers and told him, ***"I don't care what you wear when you come by to get me...as long as you keep coming by."*** She wasn't telling him to stop trying or giving him permission to do less. No, she was telling him that he, not his clothes, was what she was most interested in.

Man, my father said from that moment on, everything changed; he thought he had a winner but now, he knew. He got a part-time job and started dressing better. When he went to class, he studied harder, when he walked through town, he walked taller, when he slept, he dreamed bigger, and when he awoke, he chased those dreams harder. That one simple statement, empowered him, ignited, and lit a fire inside of him...She saw something, whatever it was, and wanted to make sure that one day, he'd see it too. More importantly, she wanted to let him know that he wasn't in it alone...

She was his girl...

He was her guy...

Hey, you might not be the best dressed, best this or best that. You might not be firm here or firm there or have all your hair or all those other things that at some point fade. But when it's all said and done...the best feeling in the world is to have someone who loves you. Someone who loves you enough to see that you're on your way to something better, even if you can't see it.

An even better feeling is knowing that they're so into you, regardless of where you stand right now or how long it might take you to get to a better place...that they're willing to wait...

As long as you to keep coming by...

The Secret and The Promise

As the years have gone by, seldom has there been a situation where my father hasn't been able to find a bright side. You get laid off from the job and call him...he says, "that just means there's a better one coming." Your car breaks down and you need to spend a chunk of cash to get it fixed... "well just be happy you had the money." Walk in with a bad haircut... "hey, it'll grow back." I promise you, that dude will spin anything into a positive...except war. He fought in Korea and Vietnam and whenever he mentions those places, those experiences, he never, ever says anything good.

Prior to his leaving on what would be his final tour of Vietnam, he and my mother sat down, and he openly discussed with her the horrors of war. The sight of men who had become more like brothers, perishing, the stifling heat of the jungles, the constant threat of an attack at all points of the day and night—he went over all that. He had cheated death so many times and here he was, being sent to cheat it one more again but this time...something inside said death would win.

She listened...and then she told him a secret...
After hearing her secret...he made her a promise...

My mother was a small woman – in stature. Even though she was small, when she entered a room, her presence was always felt; her presence spoke for her but for the longest time, even it kept a secret.

Day after day, she went about her routine, drinking coffee and having girl time with her best friends, one next door and the other three doors down. When they got together, I tell you, it was something special. One morning, she rose in a bit of pain and asked the girls if they could come by a little earlier than normal. Upon arrival, she asked if they'd mind taking her to the hospital and of course they said yes.

They loaded up the car with mom calling dibs on the back seat where she rested calmly. The driver looked back and asked how she felt to which she replied, "just fine." A few minutes passed, and the passenger peered over her shoulder and asked if she needed anything..."no, just keep going."

They kept came to a red light at which time the driver turned completely around and demanded an answer to which my mother softly replied ...

"Sweetheart...can't you see I'm having a baby?"

The secret was out...and that baby...was me.

Thousands of mile away soldiers were fighting an enemy that in most cases they couldn't see. Bullets flying, bombs bursting, bodies falling and with each occurrence the likelihood of my father returning home lowered. He told me he fought harder than ever that time and did things, took chances he never took before because he had made a promise.

He fought hard because he promised to get home to see this newborn baby girl. Yes, my parents just knew that they were going to have a girl this last time around and decided Lynn would be her name. So, when the doctor handed me to my mother and she saw that I was in fact a boy and not a girl, he offered her the chance to change the spelling of my name. "No sir" she replied. "That's the name my man and I chose, that's the way we spelled it, put it down."

I wear that name proudly and seldom does a week go by that I don't get a piece of mail addressed to "Ms. Lynn Pearcey" or "Mrs. Lynn Pearcey" instead of Mr. Lynn Pearcey. I smile, chuckle (especially when it's makeup!) Whenever I tell my father he gets a kick out of it too. I'll also stop and think to myself that somewhere up there, Mom is smiling and chuckling too...smiling, chuckling and letting me know in her own special way that even though she's on the other side, nothing can ever separate the three of us...

Nothing.

If you find a woman who can keep a secret, that special secret...keep her.
And if you find a man who is willing to fight to keep a promise...never let him go.

I'll see you Later

Over the years, I've worn several hats with my father. I was the errand boy, running down to the store for a simple purchase, making it back so fast he'd laugh and say, "I didn't even know you were gone." I was his backyard landscaper, the one who made sure the backyard looked just as good as the front … sometimes.

Before ESPN, I was his ESPN, keeping him abreast of the latest scores and making sure he knew what time the big games kicked off. I was his newspaper steward, making sure none of them were thrown out until he was finished reading them. I was his new recipe taster, his Western watching sidekick, and the one who made sure the kitchen counters were wiped down just the way he liked them. The day he came in and caught me listening to his precious jazz collection, he beamed with joy saying, "now I know who to leave my records to." At that moment, that moment when time stood still … I became his jazz loving kid.

All those and so many more were important, but my most important role, the one that stood head and shoulders above all others … was making sure he had the coolest running shoes in town. Yes, when he hit the road to "put in a few miles" as he liked to say, he did it in style thanks to yours truly. A few months back I went down to see him, sporting a new pair I was breaking in for an upcoming race. He looked down, saw them, and asked me to find him a nice pair as he was just about ready to get back out on the road.

Back home I came, on a mission for this was no ordinary purchase – this was a celebration. A celebration as the man doctors said would never walk again was ready to put on his shoes and run. To this mall and that mall, I went, searching for a pair befitting an occasion of this sort. I searched and searched for just the right shoe and then yesterday, the most beautiful thing happened …

He got his wings …

🌲 🌲 🌲

Our father passed yesterday and it's the saddest, happiest feeling I've ever felt. I'm sad because there will be no more runs to the store, recipes to taste, stories to tell or lessons to teach. He'll never get the shoes he sent me looking for and our dream of running a race together will never come to pass. Those things make me sad.

But my sad, my sorrow doesn't come close to the happy, the joy I feel because he's finally back with the one he loved the most – my mother. A long time ago when I was small, I remember a team of workers coming to our home, telling my mother that they were going to attach a fence to ours. She told them before they did, she'd have to get approval from her husband. Time and time again that day they came back until finally telling her they were going to go ahead and complete their assignment. My mother stood by that fence and told them, "I'm waiting on my man…"

She left 44 years ago and when I close my eyes and think of her, I see her standing at Heaven's gates the same way she stood at that fence so many years ago. I see angels coming over, praying with and for her, softly comforting and asking her to join them. Then I see her smiling, hugging, and thanking them before telling them … "I'm waiting on my man …" This morning, I'm happy because she doesn't have to wait any longer.

I knew he was leaving this week. When you love somebody, you just know. So, I went down and spent one last day with him. He couldn't talk, but he could hear. He could hear, so I pulled up a chair and sat there thanking him. I thanked him for staying – this time and the first time. This time he stayed to show us how to fight. The first time, he stayed to raise six children during an era when most men would've left and not thought twice about it. It was during that first time that we learned how to love.

As we sat there, me talking, him listening, I pulled out my phone and began playing some of his favorite jazz tunes – the ones he used to play around the house on the weekends. He hadn't spoken in days, but when he heard Dexter Gordon playing that sweet saxophone … his face lit up and he smiled … one last time.

One of the quirkiest things about our relationship was that we never used the word "bye" when we left each other. Instead, we always said I'll see you later. As that song played, I thought about how after every race, from 5K to a full marathon, I've ironed and folded the shirt and brought it home to him. I promised him I'd keep doing that and placing them in a special place. I told him I'll keep running toward the traffic so I can see what's coming. I made sure he knew I'd keep using that good gas, drinking water, staying away from them sodas, and eating plenty of greens.

I told him to hug my mother tight and before leaving the room, I hugged him tight one last time, bent down and whispered in his ear …

I'll see you later …

Cardinal Sightings

I love my house, love it even more now that I've really begun decorating, living in, and putting my signature on it. On the inside, it's roomy, but still intimate and that's one of the things that hit me as soon as I walked into it. But while I was smitten by the inside, if I'm being honest it was the outside that sealed the deal, more specifically the porches. Some of my fondest childhood memories took place on my parent's porches. I missed them and I promised myself that if and when I moved the one thing the new place had to have ... was porches and when I saw these, I was sold.

In the front, I can sit and soak in the energy of the neighborhood without hardly being detected. In fact, a delivery driver once dropped a package at my door as I sat quietly off to the side, staring at him as he worked, and he never noticed me. But while I like the front, let me tell you ... it's the back where the real action takes place.

It started off at breakfast my first week here when for some reason, I made enough oatmeal to feed a small army, forgetting I live alone. Instead of throwing the excess away, I decided to toss it in the backyard for the birds just as I'd seen my father do for years. If I close my eyes, I can still see him flinging rice, grits, oatmeal, and bread out on our back lawn. No sooner than it landed would a bird come graciously swooping in to claim the meal, before hurrying away.

I figured the same would happen here but to my surprise, that oatmeal sat there all day. The next morning, I came out and saw that it was gone and figured the birds finally warmed up to it. That night, I tossed a few crackers out back thinking the birds might come back again and just like before, the next morning the yard was clear. This became a part of my nightly routine ... close the blinds, turn on the porch light, throw out crackers, lock the doors, turn off the lights, go to bed.

Now, no matter how tired I am, I've always had a tough time falling asleep. So, one night I decided to grab some water and go sit out on the back porch, look at the stars and take in whatever else was the night offered ... and that's when I saw it. All this time I thought birds were eating those crackers but as it turns out ... it was gang of rabbits ... also known as bunnies. Go figure ...

Just outside my backyard sits a pond. Now, in my younger days, I could throw a rock from my backyard to that pond ... with ease I might add. During those first few months, I was content to sit on the bench off to the side, marveling at the ducks swimming and of course ... sharing a cracker or two. Well, one morning the most amazing thing happened. I opened my blinds and there on my back lawn sat a gang of ducks.

It was morning, but they weren't here for coffee – they wanted crackers. As soon as I opened the door they waddled in my direction, gobbling up everything I dropped. So, I had my marching order: ducks get crackers in the mornings, bunnies get crackers in the evenings – got it.

Here of late, things have changed. Whereas mornings were reserved for ducks and evening for bunnies, somewhere along the way communication got lost. In the mornings, the time usually reserved for ducks, ducks and bunnies are both patiently awaiting my arrival. The same can be said for the nights as both parties stand waiting for the easy meal to be shared. But wait, it gets better – there are also crow and a large swan (I think that's what it is) who pokes around from time to time. You just got to love it!

A few weeks ago, as I sat there flinging crackers, watching crow swoop in, ducks waddle, and bunnies dart to and from, I noticed a red blur off to the side. I turned and there sitting high on the fence post was a cardinal. I stared at it for what seemed like forever, all the while flinging crackers its way ... but it never moved. All this action taking place ... but the cardinal wouldn't move. It was if it were there just to preside over the activities. After dropping what felt like an entire box on the ground beneath it, I concluded cardinals must not be into crackers. So, with that, I went inside to do a little research and find out what they did like.

I found out cardinals have stronger than normal beaks and prefer a diet of corn, seeds, and berries. Interesting I thought because none of those things have ever been spread in my backyard. They're fierce and protective ... and based on the look the one I saw was giving me, you won't get any argument here. None of those things explained its' presence, so I read a little more, and stumbled upon my answer. I found out that when a cardinal appears, it's not a bird – it's a loved one visiting. They show up when you're missing them or find yourself in a moment of despair. They bring a message that simply says ... I'll always be here.

I went back out but by this time, the feeding frenzy had ended. I looked up and the cardinal that stood there so stern and resolute was also gone. I thought back to the power, intensity, strength, and force emanating from that little bird and I'm convinced ... that was my father, stopping by just to check on me.

The 15th was my birthday and that morning I awakened with plans to run 6.15 miles to coincide with the date. I set out with a good pace, but a mile in ... I began to walk. I kept walking, stopping to sit on the bench overlooking the pond. Ducks looked my way, but I had no crackers to offer and besides, they know where to find me. I realized this would be the first time in as long as I can remember, I didn't hear my father's voice telling me happy birthday. He'd always call at the crack of dawn and before hanging up, he'd remind me to keep my eye on the mailbox. Just like clockwork, on or after each birthday, there in my mailbox I'd find a puffy, white envelope, filled with newspaper ... with a crisp $100 bill hidden in it. I laughed about that and some of the other quirky little things that made him special. One year I called him out saying he only gives me that money so I can turn around and buy him a Father's Day gift. His response was a sly grin. With that my thoughts shifted to the reality that this would be my first Father's Day without him. No worries, he's in a better place.

The sun was getting high and so too was the temperature, so I figured I best be getting home. He used to always warn me not to get caught out in that sun and that day, as always, I listened. With that, I rose to my feet and to my surprise, in the tree directly in front of me ... sat a cardinal. I couldn't help but chuckle. He didn't call me that morning and he didn't drop money in the mail. I wasn't able to spend that money on his gift, but when I saw that cardinal yet again, I was comforted to know ...

My father will always be here ...

Some Things need to be Cooked

Cooking has become one of my favorite things to do, but it wasn't always that way. Yes, there was a time when my pots and pans hardly ever saw the light of day. They were for show and not go as most, if not all of my meals were sent to the microwave or received at a drive-thru window. If I wasn't doing one of those two things ... a bag of chips, cookies or some other form of junk was how I survived.

I was eating so I didn't see the problem, but my father did. I'd come home on the weekends and he'd hit me with the typical battery of questions parents have for young adults. "How's the job ... you ever hear from your old buddy from school ... you like that place you living in ... that car of yours holding up ok ..."? All these and sometimes more were asked before he finally got around to the one that mattered most to him.

"Are you eating up there"?

I assured him I was, but the way I devoured the food he prepared for me told a far different story. One day as we sat sharing a meal, he looked over at me, wiped the crumbs from his mouth and said, "I tell you what I want you to do", whenever he says that, it means listen.

He told me to make a stop at the grocery store when I arrived home, before rattling off a list of items I was to buy. Chicken, pork chops, ground beef, vegetables, rice, and a few other things. Once he was finished with the grocery list, the cooking lesson began. "Rinse off your meat, get you some salt, a little pepper season the meat up good. Next, chop up some onions and carrots, taters (potatoes) and put them to the side.

That old rascal is the master of timing, notorious for pulling rabbits out of hats, so to speak. Without any announcement, he rose up from the table, went to the back of that tiny frame house and returned ... with a Crock Pot.

"Get you a tee tee (that means a little in his language) of water, pour it in here, then put your meat and vegetables in. Cover it up, turn it on low and from time to time, come back in there and check on it. Before you know it, you'll have something good sitting in front of you".

I sat there staring at that Crock Pot. Before I could say a word, he took off his glasses, tilted his head forward and said, "you can't keep putting everything in that microwave ... some things need to be cooked ..."

Some of us, myself included, want everything in life to be microwaved. We want to start the business today, microwave it and retire tomorrow. Relationship goes cold, no worries, find a microwave throw it in and it's ready to go. The reality of our world is that the best things in life take time ... It takes time to build a stable business. It takes time to build a relationship that's strong enough to weather the storms. Raising a child, especially in this day and age, takes time.

Next time you find yourself facing one of life's challenges, instead of applying that microwave mindset that leaves you frustrated, disheartened and miserable, step back. Season that situation, put in the ingredients needed to make it just right. Walk away, but from time to time, check back on it to see how it's coming along. It's going to take time but remember if you want something good to come your way, you can't keep putting everything in the microwave.

Some things, need to be cooked ...

She Can't Take Her Eyes Off Her

I remember a whole lot about my mother even though she passed on when I was 7 and began saying goodbye when I was only 5. Things come back to me from time to time; some make me happy while others, make me sad. The happy stems from the time we had together and the sad from what we never got the chance to become. Sometimes things come in bits and pieces – at other points, they come in waves and what didn't make sense as a child make perfect sense now that I'm a man. Young or old, boy or a man, one thing I'll never forget … is her stare. It wasn't menacing but it was powerful, equal parts authoritative and nurturing. Special is the best I can describe it and although it didn't last long, it felt like forever. I promise you, when her eyes caught yours, you felt as if nothing were impossible.

When my training wheels came off, when I learned to tie my shoes, and the first time I stood up to the neighborhood bully, her stare was there. It was powerful and knew just what to say. My first trip on the school bus, I boarded with that, "I'm not coming home again" look on my face…her stare said, ***"Don't you worry little boy, I'll find you"*** …it was the best day ever.

My mother stared at my sister a lot; I mean a whole lot. I never knew why then, but as the years roll by, it's become clear. She knew her time with us was short, and she was about to leave her only girl in a house with 6 men; capable men, but none of them were women; all of them loved her dearly…but none of them were mothers.

My sister had (and still has) doubters who wonder if she can do "it" whatever "it" may be. They wondered if she would be able to survive cancer … and she beat it hands down; two forms at that. When others said her window had closed and she had too much going on to pursue a college education, she had the nerve to think otherwise and here she stands … a college graduate. Here's my favorite…the ones who wondered how she'd learn to cook…but family and friends…some of those same ones who said she'd never learn how come from miles away just to get a plate. Then they said she'd never be a good mother, "how, she barely had one herself" is what the whisper on the street was…but I challenge anyone to find one better.

People often wonder how she's able to do all these things and so much more…well, here's the secret…My mother is still staring….

And she's so proud of the woman her only daughter has become … she can't take her eyes off of her…

19

A Mother's Touch

I'm blessed. I have a house, a car, a career, a healthy mind, and a healthy body. I have good friends; no make that great friends with some being old and some being new ... all being cherished just the same. I have a wonderful family with some of those friends I mentioned actually doubling as family during certain points in my life. All these people and things I count as blessings. But without question my most valued, most treasured blessings can be found in my kitchen; two skillets, one red and one yellow that my mother purchased in Germany way back in the 1960's. Now understand, these are not just your average skillets. No. They're unique, they stand out in the crowd, they're sturdy and battle tested as evidenced by over 50 years of use...and they're simply beautiful...just like my mother.

Whenever I cook, be it morning, noon or night, chances are I'll pull out one or both of those skillets and use them to prepare my meal. I might use them to cook egg whites and turkey bacon for breakfast, fry a turkey burger for lunch or brown some meat for dinner. And after every use I wash, dry, and handle them with extreme care. I make them a priority above all other things...just like my mother did with us.

The best part of having these two skillets in my home is that each time I touch one of those handles to stir this or flip that; to clean the inside or the outside...I know my hands are touching the same places hers once touched. And each time I touch one of those handles I'm reminded of the strength of a mother's touch.

A mother's touch...you can't beat it...so don't even try...
A mother's touch can heal the deepest hurt.
A mother's touch can calm even the most violent of life's storms.
A mother's touch can fix a broken heart...by softly saying no matter who walked out...she never will.

Do yourself, and your mother, a favor today. Grab her hand and just hold it for a minute. And when you let go, watch how much better you feel. Whatever pain you felt prior to that handholding transferred it to her. Then she transferred it back to you in a message laced with love saying everything is going to be just fine.

That's what mother's do...that's what a mother's touch will do...

Mrs. Bailey

"It takes a village to raise a child." This African proverb says although a child was born to one family, raising that child is the responsibility of an entire community. With our angel getting her wings so early on, it was a blessing to grow up in a community, a village filled with people who embodied this tried and true adage, especially the mothers – the most beautiful parts of the village.

Funerals hurt – there's just no other way to put it. They represent the ending of one life and the changing of many others. Grieving never ends ... it just changes over time, manifesting itself in different ways and stages of life. Events surrounding the loss can take years to unpack, but eventually at the right time, in the right way, time releases them. My mother's best friend and I had a conversation decades after her passing. Not sure what sparked it, maybe it was just time to release it. Regardless of how it came about it's come to be one of my most cherished memories.

The night before the wake she approached the funeral home announcing that she would be putting my mother's makeup on. Yes, she– not a member of their staff – she would be the last one to touch that beautiful face. The director told her they'd never done anything of the sort in the past. ***"This time you will,"*** was her firm response.

I worked in a funeral home a long time ago for a short time, but long enough to know that allowing a family member or friend this kind of freedom could cost a director their license. As her story unfolded, I came to realize that the director wasn't focused on a license, law, or a fine – he saw love, the kind of love that can only exist between best friends.

She kept talking and I kept listening, and it became apparent that the night wasn't about makeup. It was about one last laugh at each other, with each other ... one last lean up against the fence that separated their houses. A final yell from her porch, telling her best friend how much she meant to her, how much she'd be missed and promising to be there whenever we called. Over the years, she never missed a chance to speak about the special bond they shared. I can still hear her saying, "your mama was something else", laughing and smiling every step of the way.

She kept a picture of my mother on her living room mantle, the same picture I carry in my wallet. Behind that picture of mom in my wallet, sits a picture of her best friend. Every time I open it and look at them, I imagine them up above, leaning on the fence, yelling from the porch, sharing a good laugh … still being best friends.

At some point, life will force us all to get in a hurry. But no matter how big of a hurry you find yourself in, take your time loving on your mother because one day she won't be here to love. A phone call, lunch, dinner, however you choose to celebrate her, do it while you still can. Savor it and soak up every last drop. But in between loving on her, send a little love toward those other mothers in your life … A sister, a mother-in-law, an aunt, or a best friend …

They're the most beautiful parts of the village.

Westerns

Aside from football one of my father's favorite things to watch is a good, old-fashioned Western. Westerns are his thing and when my mother was alive, it was one of her favorite ways to rib him. I can still hear her saying, "Come Saturday no matter what, somehow, some kind of way, your daddy is going to find him a Western." Now, to put this into perspective, back in those days we only had 6 or 7 channels to choose from as this was well before the emergence of cable television--so it actually was quite the accomplishment.

As quiet as it was kept, I was just as fond if not fonder of Westerns and nowadays, I find myself flipping through channels looking for one. It's a lot easier with hundreds of channels to choose from but at some point, in every weekend, you'll find me perched in front of my television, watching … a Western.

No matter the storyline, the plot, the number of good guys or bad guys, one thing every Western has…is a horse. No matter where the characters go…to town…to the bank…to the feed store…to visit a friend…or home, there's always a horse involved. And where there's a horse, there's always a horse post…that flimsy structure positioned out front.

Every Cowboy would tie his horse to a post when he dismounted but what I always found so interesting is that he never actually bothered to tie a real knot; he simply threw the reins over the post…but that horse would stay right there. That horse, powerfully built, bristling with muscle, weighing in some cases nearly a quarter of a ton, with enough strength to destroy the building that stood before them…never moved.

It wasn't the knot that kept the horse in place because remember, a real knot was never tied. The horse didn't stay put because it wasn't strong enough, nothing of the sort because horses are renowned for their strength. They were big enough and strong enough to smash that post and everything around it to pieces…so what held it in place you ask…

Their minds…their minds held them in place because those horses were never able to wrap their minds around the incredibly awesome amount of power they wielded.

So, they stayed put.

Some of us have been tied to a post for years. Oh, we're big and strong, well-educated, and say all of the right things...But the reason we stay tied to that flimsy post in whatever shape, form, or fashion it shows up day in and day out, is because we've fallen in love, with the idea that the post...is stronger than we are. We've never stepped back and wrapped our mind around the incredible power we wield in life -- so we stay put.

Friend my hope for you today is that you dare to harness and then unleash the true gifts, the vast amounts of potential that you've been blessed with and walk boldly into your best you...but in order for all that to start...

You must first...free your mind...

Things You Learn When You Move

I recently moved from the house I had lived in for over 18 years. When I wake up and look around or walk in and see the new surroundings, I'm still in shock. I lived in that house longer than anywhere else in my life—including my childhood home so I guess the shock was to be expected. It was a long time coming and I must admit—I learned a lot when I moved...

Let go... The day I made up my mind to leave, I started packing everything. Over the next couple of months, you should have seen me. Pots and pans went into boxes, pictures came off walls, drawers were emptied, and the contents were also boxed. Yes, I packed everything. So, when the time came to finally leave, I looked around at all those boxes, called a mover and then I realized...there's no point in moving if I'm going to take everything with me because for where I was going, those things didn't fit...so I let go.

At certain points in your life, you'll move in your career, relationships...or a new house. When you do understand that everything...and everybody won't fit where you're going...so whatever or whoever it is...let go.

Never let them go...as I packed, I stumbled across a ticket stub from the 1988 movie, "Do the Right Thing." Man, oh man I remember like it was yesterday two of my closest friends and I sat in a theater in Austin watching that groundbreaking piece of work. After it was over, we discussed it over a meal, went out, laughed, joked, and did the things college kids do. A few short years later, one of those guys I spent that special day with passed on. As I held that ticket stub, I thought back to that and all the other good times we shared...and smiled, inside and outside

Sometimes the people who matter the most in life get called to the next one before you're ready to see them leave. Just because they leave, doesn't mean they're gone. So, when you move, be sure to pack them too—not in a box but in a special part of your heart...and never let them go...

One room at a time...this new place fits me better but it's not much bigger. It's not much bigger but without many of my old things, I'm essentially starting over. Decorating a house can be fun...but it can also be daunting. Yes, it can be daunting...but I'm taking the advice of my sister. She said, "Don't get in a hurry, go slow on purpose, enjoy the process and decorate one room at a time. Slowly but surely, it'll come together."
Decorating a house is a lot like decorating a life...it works better when you slow down and enjoy the process. Planning is great but when you live on purpose, one day at a time, you'll be amazed at how slowly but surely your life will come together.

If I were you...before the "for sale" sign went up, only a handful of people knew about my plans. Once the sign went up, what was once a sea of support from family and friends was met with streams of doubt as others began to chime in. One of those others cautioned me about this thing and the other, asking if I knew what I was getting into, if I were sure about this and that, on and on. Then he said those four magic words, "If I were you." He isn't me and that's why what I was doing didn't make sense to him. When you finally decide to move, there'll be people who doubt you, caution you, question you—people who say, "If I were you." They're not you and never will be that's why what you're doing won't make sense to them...Thank them for their advice...but keep moving...

Make Mama Proud... The first thing I see when I walk out of my room or walk into my house is a sign that says, "Make Mama Proud." Each day I strive to do that. Some days I do better than others but each day, I'm trying. I think the world would be a better place if we all lived by that mantra so today do something special and make your mama proud.

Remember the ones who were there...I'm a list guy. That's right, each day I make a list of things I want to get done. During the 90's, my sister and I lived together before she transferred for work. With her moving, there were things I'd have to buy, so I made a list. Well, she found the list and wrote me a letter assuring me that she would take care of everything on it. I smiled at her offer; it warmed my heart, but I promised her I could handle it and I did.

I found that letter when I was packing. I read it and read it and then read it some more and each time I realized just how much a part of this move she was. If she hadn't opened her apartment to me when my financial aid fell through, if she hadn't picked me up from work at 1 in the morning when I didn't have a car, if dinner wasn't ready when I came home from class...this move wouldn't be happening. When you move...remember the ones who were there...they made this possible.

Small victories are victories too...I played a little football in high school...wide receiver was my position. My best game saw me "torch" the Austin Anderson secondary for three catches including a 60-yard touchdown. It was only a scrimmage but hey...I'll take it!

Well, I came across the sweatbands I wore in that game while packing. I put them on and thought back to that day. Yes, it was only a scrimmage but for that moment while I had those sweatbands on, I drifted back to that day and remembered how good it felt. In life you win some and you lose some but today, focus on the small victories. A 2-pound weight loss, a pay increase, your teen passing their drivers test. They might be small...but they're victories too...

When you move there are certain things and certain people that can't go with you and some you should never leave behind. There are some who will doubt you but remember the ones who helped make it all possible. Some days you'll question yourself but, on those days, remember the small victories. Live one day at a time and be brave enough to answer the call...Don't just stand there...make your mama proud...

Move...

Things I learned in a Fire

I was involved in a fire once and let me tell you, once was enough. I don't wish that on my worst enemy and I don't want to go through that again. It's an experience like no other, awe-inspiring is the best way I can describe it. The night of that fire changed my perspective on life. I was afraid...I worried a lot, but most of all...

I learned a lot.

Know what matters: When the fireman kicked my door in and began screaming for me to leave, I didn't know what to think. Was it real, a fire...how could this be? The day, up until that point, was perfect. We stared at each other for a moment before he begged me to get whatever I could and leave because the fire was heading my way; fast. I still wasn't convinced that this was happening, so I darted downstairs to see for myself and sure enough, it was.

Back up the stairs I went to get whatever I could. I did a quick inventory of pictures, books, CD's, a television, a stereo, nice clothes...all of them were just things. That's when I realized none of those things would matter—if I didn't have me. So, I left. When the fires of life come your way, and they will, remember things come and go—so do people. Don't lose yourself trying to hold onto things and people that the fire was sent to take away. Know what matters.

Leave.

Friends indeed: After the fire, the time came for me to move. As fate would have it, the fire stopped just shy of my building, but the heat was so intense that it damaged the foundation of the structure. As a result, it was deemed too dangerous to occupy...so I had to move. No worries, I've got friends. I called the one who was so happy to ride in my new car when I got it. I left a message, explaining the events and my needs: no call back. Next, I called that friend who was quick to ask for a loan but oh so slow to pay it back...never heard from him.

Frustrated, I placed a couple more calls and bingo...I found a pair willing to help. Here's the thing— one showed up wearing a back brace as he had been in an auto accident a few days earlier. The next day, the other drove over in his brother's truck because his car was in the shop...but both showed up.

During certain phases of your life, you'll find yourself in spaces that are no longer fit to be occupied because the heat from what you were dealing with may have damaged the very foundation. Those are the times you'll need a friend to talk to...to lean on...to be there...to pick you up.

Remember the ones you called who heard but you never heard from, the ones who've leaned on you but never offered a shoulder for you to do the same: the ones you were there for but when given the opportunity, they weren't there for you. Most importantly never forget the ones who answered, stood tall, listened and no matter what it took, showed up.

Those are your true friends.

Sometimes, you must stay: As I ran down the stairs that night, living a nightmare on a day that had until that point been a dream, I wanted nothing more than to get in my car and drive away—but life had other ideas.

Yes, the life had other ideas. The fire department had set up shop on the hood of my car using it as a de facto command center. I wanted to leave but I had no choice but to stay...so I did. All night and well into the morning I watched my complex burn one building at a time. Each time one burned, I thought how blessed I was to make it out.

When life begins to burn, you'll want to turn and leave...but chances are, life will have other ideas. Because in some cases, the only way you'll ever realize just how blessed you are...is to watch everything around you, except you, burn to the ground.

Stay.

The sound: I never knew fire made a sound. Up until that point I'd never been around one, so I just assumed it was a silent monster that simply ravaged everything in its path. That night as I ran downstairs, I remembered hearing this rushing sound. Curious, I looked around the corner and realized that noise was actually coming from the fire. I stood there for what seemed like forever and listened...to this day, whenever I drift back in my mind, I can still hear that sound.

When you go through the trials of life, the fires if you will...take time to listen. More importantly, never forget what you heard.

That thing I needed most was looking for me: So, they finally doused the flames, but I had no place to go. This was new to me so; I went out and bought a few things and checked into a hotel. I missed a couple days on the job and when I got back, I'd leave a little early to go look at other apartments but each night, back to that hotel room I returned.

Then one day I got a call at work from the manager of my complex. She said, they had an extra unit that I could live in until another one became available. All this time I was out looking for a place to live and a place to live was looking for me...I just had to slow down enough to be found.

28

My father once told me that when you're out there looking for something, chances are that same something is out there looking for you. You've just got to be wise enough to know when to slow down.

When life starts to burn, you'll want to leave but sometimes the best thing you can ever do is stay. But when you stay, be sure to listen; listen closely and never forget what you heard.

The time will come to move on, in search of something better, a good thing, but understand that something better, that good thing...is also searching for you... When you come out on the other side, you won't have to wonder who your friends are. They'll be standing there, waiting to help you pick up the pieces. It'll get hot but through it all, you'll find out which things and which people to take and which things and which people to leave behind.

And no matter what you lose, you'll learn the lesson that you really are your best thing.

Real Man 101

Back in 2018 when his health challenges became more prevalent, my father made the decision to give me medical power of attorney. This move granted me the authority to make all his end of life medical decisions, but before we signed the paperwork, there were a couple of caveats. "No resuscitating – if I start to go, let me go." I nodded in agreement, promising to honor that wish. "I don't want all those tubes running through me either man." "Understood", was my response and with that, we executed the document.

Fast forward a couple of years and I received the call telling me the time had come to make that dreaded end of life medical decision. "Your father is ready to transition Lynn – we just need to get the go ahead from you." I took a deep breath then asked for a few minutes to speak with my siblings. Once that was done, I called and gave the nurse my consent. Before hanging up I asked how long it would take as the last thing I wanted was for him to suffer.

"It varies from person to person, but I wouldn't be surprised if he's bright-eyed and bushy tailed this time tomorrow because this man right here ... always finds a way."

For as long as I live, I'll never forget the mix of emotions my father's face held the night he told us our mother was gone. There was hurt, pain, sorrow, grief – even a tinge of fear. As I got older and we began talking about relationships, I remember him telling me sometimes in life, you only get that "one". The "one" who makes your cloudy days sunny, the "one" who lights up the darkest night and when things get bad, just having them by your side makes everything better. She was his and he had just lost her, and he was hurting, he was afraid. That was the only time I ever saw him cry. But even through his tears I knew he would find a way.

Cooking was a challenge those first few years. I can recall many nights, he'd turn, place plates in front of us and say, "it might not look good, but give it a try." He was right. The meals didn't look good, but they tasted just fine. As the years went by, the look caught up with the taste and we had before us our very own chef, capable of making anything our hearts desired. Cakes, pies, puddings, if you can name it chances are, he made it – and made it well. But here's the thing. Our neighborhood was filled with magnificent mothers, magnificent cooks. Any of those women would've gladly stepped in and made meals for us ... but he knew that was his responsibility ... so he found a way.

I didn't get to experience the fullness of my parent's relationship. By the time I was five, she was already fighting cancer and becoming less and less of herself. So, since I didn't see much of it, I lived it through him and his loving collection of memories. They ran a tight ship – he was the provider and she was the manager. He told me several times he'd rush home with a bright idea about this or that – bright ideas that cost money. She'd listen, break out the pencil and paper, do the math and decide if whatever his bright idea was worked within the framework of the life they were building. Sometimes it was yes, sometimes it was no, sometimes it was not right now, but he always trusted her judgement, knowing that their family was at the heart of her decision.

Years later when she left, the duties of deciding which bright ideas to pursue fell squarely on his shoulders. In the beginning he was lost, but as time went on, he got better. He got better because he replayed all those nights when they sat together making decisions for them. During those times, he listened to his wife because by his own admission, her plan was better. So, when the time came for him to make decisions in her absence, he called upon the wisdom she left behind ... and that's when things got better. He said that piece of his journey taught him that when a man is in the dark being humble enough to listen to the woman by his side can be the light that helps him find his way.

When the time came for me to go away to college, I had my list of schools – none of which he could afford. The summer was coming to an end and fees and registration were looming, so he sent me on a vacation to see my brother in Miami. What I didn't know was that he had already made plans for me to go to a local community college ... in Miami. He knew he couldn't afford to send me to the places I wanted to go, but he also knew that for me to live the life he envisioned, I needed to go to college ... So, he found a way ...

Years later I stood ready to purchase my first home, but those plans hit an unexpected snag. The bank wanted me to pay off my truck – the truck that still had the new car smell. I couldn't do it, but my father could ... so he became my way.

Over the years, especially these precious last few, we've reminisced about holidays, birthdays, back to school shopping, and a number of different life touchstones. He opened up and told me how some of those things almost never happened. I had no idea. What I learned from those conversations is that when a man is finding his way, it's his duty to shield those around him until he does.

My father lasted a little less than a day when his transition began. I like to think Heaven came over and lovingly wrapped its arms around him and said, "this way." If you have a real man, not just a man, in your life, spend a little extra time honoring, loving, and appreciating him.

A real man who when there were more plates at the table than food in the pots ... rose to the occasion and made sure everybody left with a full belly. A real man, the kind who when faced with more days in the month than money in his pocket, made ends meet. A real man, one who humbles himself enough to know that in times of extreme darkness, she, the woman by his side was put there to be his light. A real man, the kind who takes spears and arrows that cause him to bleed, bend, and break on the inside, but when you look his way, he's standing tall with armor shining brightly.

Love on and adore that real man because every time life told him there wasn't one to be had...

He always found a way ...

The House Key

When I started school, my mother and I had a ritual. When the bus rounded the corner onto my street, she'd be standing there waiting for me. We'd embrace, look both ways and then run across the street to our house. She'd give me the key, I'd place it in the door, open it and we'd walk in and enjoy our time together before my siblings made it home. This ended abruptly at the age of 7 when she passed.

After grieving for a week or so, we all had to get back to trying to live which also meant going back to school. The morning of the first without her, my father put that same key that my mother and I used so many times on a piece of string and placed it around my neck. I was the youngest so I got out of school the earliest which meant I would be home first so it stood to reason that I would be the one holding that key.

That first day came and I got off the bus and realized my mother was no longer with me. I looked across the street and the one-story frame house that was so warm and welcoming in times past and all of a sudden, it looked like a monster. I was no match for it so instead of going in, I sat alone on the porch and waited for my siblings. When one arrived, I'd pass them the key, they'd open the door and in the house we went. This went on for the better part of I'd say a month as I was convinced that I simply couldn't open that door without my mother.

One school afternoon, I sat there on the porch in the last outfit she bought me. I thought to myself, ***"I've dressed so well today it's like she never even left me"*** ... and that's when it hit me; she was still here. I started thinking about all of the positive things she'd say to me during our time together and how valued she made me feel regardless of the circumstances; all the loving parts of her that were still here. I started thinking about how knowingly or unknowingly, she had prepared me for this moment...and I wasn't going to let her down. I hopped up, took a deep breath, and put our key; that's what we called it, our key, in the lock, turned it and walked in.

Even though it happened over 40 years ago, I still lean on and gain strength from that moment.

You'll have days when you feel as though you're all alone. On the porch standing in front of a door you can't walk through. But here's the important thing to remember – if you're there, you're there for a reason. You're there for a reason and everything you need to open it lies within you. Sure, you can pass the key and let someone else open it for you. But always letting someone else open the door will keep you from being the person you were meant to be.

Great man, great woman, hop up today in honor of your mother, take a deep breath, put the key in the lock and open whatever door you stand before.

I promise you, there's something beautiful waiting for you on the other side....

33

Baby ... HE knows the way

It seems like yesterday when I was saying goodbye to classmates and celebrating the end of my very first school year...and that first goodbye was my most memorable. Although I grew up with an elementary school directly across the street from my home most of the children in my neighborhood were bussed to a school on the other side of town. We never really got a clear understanding of why, but my guess is that it had something to do with desegregation.

Well, when that final school bell rang, we ran to the bus and began boarding it; just like we had done hundreds of times before. *I couldn't wait to get off that bus and jump into the safe arms of my mother!* That old bus driver closed the door and we started out. It was a clear sunny day, without a cloud in the sky, with a soft breeze flowing through those slightly opened bus windows. Everything was going great...until the bus driver took an unexpected turn.

Now, at 5-years-old, my exposure to the city was limited. Limited though it may have been, by the end of the school year I had memorized that bus route home, so much so that in my little mind I guess I had come to believe that it was the only way. So, when the bus driver detoured that day, I promise you my whole life...all 5 years and 11 months of it...passed before my eyes. He made turn after turn and with each one I became more and more convinced that I would never make it home. At every single stop he made I fought the urge to jump out of that big yellow bus and find my way home on my own.

Suddenly, things started to look a little familiar...and I became hopeful! He made one more right turn and there standing on the right side of the street...was my mother waiting patiently at the bus stop like she had done every day that year. When I got off the bus, I started telling her how worried I was because the bus driver didn't take the "right way." She listened patiently and when I was done, I remember her smiling, chuckling, and softly saying, "Baby, he knows the way."

Have you ever found yourself wondering if God has you headed in the right direction? You ever get discouraged because the bus He has you on is taking a way that looks nothing like the way you thought you should be going? The next time you 're in this type of a situation, fight the urge to jump off at the next stop; stay on and ride the bus because eventually, He will get you to the right destination.

The route you take might not look like you thought it would, might not look anything like it did all those other times but rest assured baby...

He knows the way...

The Whole Note

Even though it's been almost two years, I tell you, it's still hard to believe I moved. I mean I spent the better part of 18 years at that first house and from time to time, I toyed with moving, but never saw it happening – until it did. These last few weeks we've become so much better acquainted and with each passing day, I learn to love it more than the day before. Yes, this downtime has allowed me to connect with this house, but it's also given me the chance to reflect on the unexpected blessing I received many years ago …

The one that allowed me to walk into … my first house.

I had just turned 30 and I decided I was done renting; that's right, I was ready to become a homeowner. With that, I selected a realtor – who just so happened to be a good friend, and this new chapter of life began unfolding. Weekend after weekend we searched and searched, from sunup to sundown, until we finally found the right one.

We made an offer, the builder accepted and the countdown to homeownership began. Each night instead of going to home to my apartment, I'd drive over to that house, stand in the front yard, and make plans. I'll do this over here, put this type of plant there, this picture in that room … on and on.

Everything was going just as planned then out of nowhere, the builder called with news no applicant wants to hear. Seems the bank, the one that previously marveled at my credit rating, income, and debt ratio now had concerns. He said the only way I could get financing, was if I paid off my truck … the same truck that had over four years left on the note.

Frustrated, I called my father to vent as he always had a way of making things better. I told him the story about five or six different ways, maybe more and each time he patiently listened … five or six different ways. – maybe more After the last version, I paused, leaving an opening for him to finally speak.

"You done", he asked. "Yeah, I'm done Daddy, thanks for listening" was my reply.
"Well, what time can you pick me up." Confused I asked, "Pick you up from where Daddy? What's going on?" Without hesitating he said, "I got to get up there and pay that truck off for you man. So, what time can you come by and get me?" I backed the conversation up thinking maybe he misunderstood the situation.

"Daddy … they're not asking me to make a monthly payment, they're asking me to pay the entire loan off." No sooner than I was done talking, did he start. "I heard you now what time you coming down here man?"

I stalled and that's when he stopped asking ... and started telling. "Be at my house tomorrow at 9 and let's get this business handled." End of conversation. I showed up just like I was told and there he was. Yeah man, there he was standing in what I affectionately called ... his Daddy Uniform -- a baseball cap, buttoned down shirt tucked into starched jeans with his glasses in the front shirt pocket, a rolled-up newspaper in the back jean pocket, topped off by a slightly worn pair of running shoes. "Let's boogie" he yelled, and with that we began our three-hour trip back to Dallas.

He paid the truck off and we were back in Killeen by 6 that evening. I thanked him a million times and before leaving I thanked him again with a hug. As we broke our embrace, he grabbed me by the shoulders, looked me square in the eyes, popped me upside the head with his newspaper and softly whispered, ***"I've been wanting to bless you!"***

Here's the thing. I didn't call looking to get my truck paid off. Even in my wildest dreams that dream never would've crossed my mind. I just needed to talk. Fact is, I had already spoken to my apartment complex about signing another lease and cancelling the home purchase altogether. But when I talked to my father, things changed.

Even with all the turmoil swirling around, I felt a certain calmness on that call. These last few days I've come to realize that feeling came from simply being in his presence, being in the presence of my father. I smile (and I know he's smiling too!) as I remember trying to convince him it was more than he could handle ... only to have him remind me of who I was dealing with. And as long as I live, I'll never forget the sincerity in his eyes when he said he had been wanting to bless me.

He's often the most neglected member of the family, but during this time when we're all focused on one another, don't forget to love on and talk to your father. A phone call, a cup of coffee, a conversation on the porch, working in the yard or any way you choose. Make it a point to talk to and when this storm passes, continue talking to your father.

Because when you do ... things change.

A Christmas Story

I love everything about Christmas. I love the houses adorned with lights, the malls with people bustling about, the commercials creatively selling their sales -- I love all those things and much, much more. When it comes to gifts, I've begun to live that old axiom that says it's better to give than to receive. Yes, at this point, I'm more giver than receiver and I'm just fine with that dynamic. I'm just fine with that because every Christmas morning, my heart opens the gift I received the year I thought this special day would no longer be special.

It's the gift that keeps on giving.

The first Christmas without my mother just didn't feel like Christmas. I mean no matter how hard we tried, without her in the mix, we couldn't get anything right. The tree was off, the decorations lacked pop and an unshakable chill stood in the places her heart once warmed. The food, the spirit ... the cheer, nothing and I mean nothing felt right.

Even the gifts seemed a bit off without her there to manage that process. Oh, everyone got gifts and we were grateful for them but at that point, my father was a provider – not a nurturer so the gifts we got were practical, not fun. It was a tough day, but we made the best of it and kept going.

The year moved on and so did we, but the sour taste of that first Christmas without her hung heavy in our home and hearts. Experiences like these had come to be our new normal – but we also held onto precious gems from the past – gems like wishing on stars. Yes, one of our favorite rituals when she was alive was to sit on the back porch, look up and wish on stars. On a warm summer night, one of my brothers sat us down on that same porch, we looked up and began casting wishes and let me tell you, it felt so good.

My sister pointed to a star and wished for a sewing machine at Christmas so she could sew just like mom used to. Following her lead, I picked a star and wished for a Christmas bicycle so I could ride with all the other kids in the neighborhood. We stayed back there for what seemed like forever, laughing, smiling, joking, and doing innocent things kids our age did – and her presence was right there with us. We eventually went into the house, leaving those wishes with those stars – or so we thought.

We blinked and before we knew it summer and fall had passed, and Christmas Day had arrived again. That morning my brother eagerly roused my sister and I from our sleep, ushered us down the hallway, clicked on the light ... and there before us ... stood a sewing machine ... and a brand-new bicycle! How'd this happen we thought? Instinctively we ran to our father ... he shook his head ... and pointed to our brother.

By this time, my brother was 16 years old and working. He worked double-shifts, overtime, and saved lunch money to make sure those wishes didn't stay with those stars. He worked double-shifts, overtime, and saved his lunch money ... to make sure his sister and brother had the type of Christmas his mother would've wanted for them.

Hiding Christmas gifts is something everyone has done a time or two ... but how do you hide a sewing machine and bicycle? I mean in a small frame house like ours gifts like that would've easily been found. He knew this, so he enlisted the help of a beautiful family a couple houses over. They graciously opened their home, allowing him to store our gifts there until just the right time. As the years have gone by, every time I pass their home, every time I speak to anyone from that family the first thing that comes to mind ... is the role they played in making that day so truly special. They're gifts too.

I'm more giver than receiver now and I don't know if I'll get anything for Christmas ever again and I'm fine with that. I'm fine with that, because I'll always be able to close my eyes, open my heart and unwrap the precious memory of that special Christmas.

It's the gift that keeps on giving.

Tulsa

Friday's are usually light days for me but that was not the case one week as I was stacked with a full day of meetings. The first part was spent in Dallas and by the afternoon I found myself sitting in downtown Fort Worth but only after stopping in a couple of places in between. Hey, no complaints here as meeting shows that someone out there sees some value in the services I offer.

As the final meeting wrapped the client cocked her head and inquired about the name of my business. She asked, "If your last name is Pearcey and you own the company why did you name it The Coley Group? Shouldn't it be The Pearcey Group?" I explained that I wear my father's last name with pride. But I went on to tell her that I decided on the name Coley because that was my mother's maiden name...and she was from Tulsa, Oklahoma.

That inspires me.

Years after their emancipation African Americans were quasi-bound; no longer a slave but not fully recognized as being free. This went on for decades but as the nation continued to expand so too did the horizons of the former slaves which led many of them to the newly formed state of Oklahoma.

They arrived in Tulsa saying all they needed was a chance and when they were finally given one...oh my God. In less than 15 years and in the midst of segregation the African American community of Greenwood was formed. It was a community in the truest sense of the term filled with entrepreneurs from every pursuit, bursting with love and power. There were doctors, lawyers, dentists, dry cleaners, bus lines, schools, hospitals, and stores of all types. It came to be known as The Black Wall Street with an economy that was so strong that it took a single dollar one year before it cycled out of that community. To put that into context, it takes a dollar less than one hour to cycle out of the black community today.

The Greenwood community of Tulsa, Oklahoma was everything the world said the black man, the black woman, the black child, the black family could never be. But everyone wasn't smiling. For years members of the local KKK watched helplessly as Greenwood thrived looking for a reason to bring it down and on May 31st, 1921...they got it. A young black man brushed up against a young white girl, he only brushed up against her...but that was all they needed.

What ensued has come to be known as the most underreported act of terrorism the world has ever known. An angry mob led by the KKK descended upon Greenwood with the mandate to kill anything black. Before they came, they cut phone lines to ensure no communications would go out and no help could get in. Some came by foot, some by horse and wagon, some drove and some...came by plane as crop dusters were flown over and homemade bombs were dropped on Greenwood.

When it ended on June 1st, when all the shooting of black residents, the looting of their homes, the killing of their babies and the burning of years of hope that would have provided fuel for generations to come had ended...the promise of Tulsa still stood.

At certain points whatever and wherever we have all thought about quitting. I know I have. There have been several instances in life where I thought about just quitting. From personal to professional and points in between ... I've thought about quitting... but then I remembered Greenwood. Hey, anyone can keep going on the good days. But on your bad ones, brother, or sister before giving up, whatever and wherever it might be look to your what and your why and remember the promise of Tulsa because it still stands...

That ought to inspire someone.

The Baby's Crying … Again

One of my life's greatest disappointments is that I never brought a child home to my father. He always thought I'd make a great parent and I would've loved to have gifted him with another grandchild but, as the old saying goes, some things just aren't meant to be. But while I don't have any children, all my friends do and over the years I've lived the life of a parent through the stories they've shared.

I remember one telling me how proud he felt the day he and his wife brought their first child home. He said all day, they huddled over the little bundle, staring in amazement … attending to his every need … making sure that child knew they were there. He said even when the baby drifted off to sleep … they sat with eyes fixated on that little life of theirs in utter disbelief.

Night fell and they retreated to bed and so too did the newest member of their family. They were all sleeping soundly when out of nowhere … the baby began to cry! No worries there as they both jumped up, trampling one another, speeding down the hall … eager to attend to him. They rocked him back to sleep … stared some more before eventually retreating back to finish their rest.

As the days progressed, that baby continued crying at night, but unlike the early parts of their parenting journey when they showed up as a team … now, they took turns. "It's your night … it's your night … I got to get up early … so do I …" They went back and forth like this for a while and a funny thing happened … the baby fell back to sleep. This became the norm; the baby would cry at night the parents would open their eyes ever so slightly before reminding themselves that he'd fall back to sleep.

More time passed and that baby still cried, but along the way, he had learned to climb, scoot, and crawl. So, now instead of just sitting there crying unattended, ignored, and eventually falling back to sleep, he became bold. That's right he became bold, climbed out of his bed, and made his way down to his parent's room.

My boy said the look on that baby's face the first time he did it said it all. It said "you used to come check on me when you heard me crying. You'd pick me up … rock me back to sleep and even as I slept, I could still feel your presence. But when you found out I'd fall back to sleep, you stopped coming. His little face said, "so since you started ignoring me, here I am … interrupting your intimacy … disrupting your rest … causing you to put your favorite show on pause … forcing you to finish that book another time."

His face went on to say … "I'll keep crying because I want you to hear me, but unlike those times before when I cried in my room and fell back to sleep, now I'm in your room." The face turned stern and said, "oh and one more thing. Remember, I didn't ask to be here, it was you who brought me here. I'm awake … and no matter what you do, I plan on keeping you awake …"

"Until you deal with me …"

The names change, but the pattern never does. Sandra Bland, Michael Brown, Trevon Martin, Freddie Gray … Tamir Rice … and this time, it's George Floyd. They're murdered, we get mad, chant their names, create catchy taglines, t-shirts, and hashtags and flood social media. We march … or protest, whichever you prefer, which leads to impromptu speeches given by impromptu leaders. We do all this, and the nation listens as we cry. The nation gets up, runs down the hall in unison to check on Black America … to see why he's crying. This goes on for a few days and then one day, without notice… they stop coming. We keep crying, but the nation stops coming because they know eventually, just like that baby crying in the night, we'll fall back to sleep.

After watching that poor brother begging for his life this time has to be different – this time, we have to be bold. Bold enough to do more than cry, bold enough to scoot, climb, crawl, or do whatever needs to be done to make it to America's room. When we get there, look at them and say, "you used to check on me when you heard me crying … with your cameras, papers, and shows. You stopped coming, but I'm still hurting … so, now I'm here."

To interrupt your intimacy by reminding you that I have over $1 trillion worth of spending power …

I'll disrupt your rest … by casting my vote for someone who understands lives like mine really do matter…

I want to remind you it's past time for this country to have a new favorite show – one where everybody gets equal airtime…

And about that book I'm forcing you to put down, you can pick it up again, but first … let's include a chapter about my people …

And one last thing. Remember, I didn't ask to be here. I was brought here in the most horrific of ways and to pay homage to those who came before me, I'm staying awake. More importantly, I plan on keeping you awake ...

Until you deal with me...

Mr. Hornsby

The cool thing about the neighborhood I grew up in, well make that one of the cool things because there were so many, was that I didn't have to go far to get to my best friends. Just a few doors this way or that way or a walk across my street or the next one over and I was there. Back then, unlike today, kids actually played outside of the home. From pickup basketball games to bike riding, baseball, and sandlot football; we actually came and played outside and had the best times doing it.

Around that time households were run a little differently too. Today, a child can meet any and everybody due to advances in technology, nothing stopping them. When I was growing up, in order to get to a child, you first had to go through their parent. This was true with the phone, but it was especially true if you came by their houses as children, especially children in my house, were not allowed to just take off running toward the door when the doorbell rang. As far as I can recall, this same rule held true for all the homes of my best friends.

Now no matter how close my friends and I grew to be, at certain times all of our parents would answer the door with that "you again" look on their face...with the exception of this one house. The kid who lived there was kind of cool and so was I so I figured we might have something. We'd catch up on the playground to shoot hoops, toss a ball or any number of things kids our age did. Then one day I decided instead of waiting for this kid to arrive at the playground, I'll just go and ring his doorbell.

As was the case with the other houses, his father answered the door. Let me tell you he greeted me like I was a long-lost friend who he hadn't seen in years. The next day I stopped by and just like he had done the day before, his father joyfully greeted me! The third day came, and I rang the doorbell and just as he had been on those other two days, there stood that father, with that same greeting. As the third day ended and I made my way back home I thought to myself, "Poor guy must have forgotten that I had been there for two days in a row."

I grew older and so too did my friend and each time I came over there was the father...there was that greeting. On one visit it dawned on me that it wasn't that he had forgotten I'd come by the day before or the day before that. His memory worked well, better than most. No, he greeted me the way he did because he was so happy to see me again.

Years went by and a funny thing happened. That parent the one who greeted me at the door, he too became my friend. Whenever I would come home to visit my father, he would make sure I never left town without first stopping by to say hello. Sometimes the visits were short and other times they were long, but each time I arrived he met me with the same joy; arms opened wide; heart opened wider.

As a boy trying to become a man and a man trying to become better, the way you listened and the simple yet precious pieces of yourself you gave...I'll always treasure them. I'm going to keep coming home of course but sadly, you won't be there now.

You're on the other side now and one day, I'll be in that same place. And when I get there something tells me you'll be at the door waiting to greet me.

And I'll be so happy to see you again...

Until then, rest well old friend...

Charlton

I grew up in a small town but, there was always something fun to do – especially in the summer. You had swimming and who doesn't like taking a dip in the pool during the hot Texas summer? Next … the arcade … yes, the arcade with spaceships, aliens, wild animals, and junk food galore! The pool and arcade were nice, but hands down the best fun was going to the mall. But, here's the catch, the mall was the best option … but only if you had a ride.

From our neighborhood to the mall was a little over a mile. Walking to the mall in the brutal Texas heat was a proposition no one wanted to sign up for … but there were times it happened. One afternoon, three of us decided to make the trek. We set out and were only a few paces in when a horn blow. We looked left in unison and there was the older brother of another friend, and he just so happened to be heading to the mall. "Need a ride?" Crisis avoided, we piled in and off we went.

We arrived a minute later, but off to the side we noticed a situation. Police officers were holding court with a group of young black boys. "I wonder what that's all about", said the driver. A law student at the time, I knew he wasn't going to let that go. Black boys alone in the company of police officers is a chilling thought – even today, so imagine what it must've felt like some 30 years ago. It might look like nothing, but we all know how quickly nothing can turn to something when black boys and police officers get together. ***"Don't worry … he'll go back", my inside voice whispered.***

We parked, poured out of the car, and hurriedly began making our way. The chatter was lively … but the driver didn't participate – instead, he walked along silently … reflective. That little voice inside said, "watch what I tell you … he's going back." We kept walking, pausing at a busy crosswalk, allowing a car or two to pass. "Trust me … he's going back" … the voice inside assured me.

The mall entrance was upon us now, and I began wondering if I was losing my mind. Just then, the voice inside calmly said "how about you focus on that $5 burning a hole in your little pocket. That situation in the parking lot will be just fine … he's going back." Then it happened…

"I'll see you guys later. I'm going back to check on those boys."

I'm not sure what I did with that $5 or where it was spent. Pizza, fries, video games … I forgot a long time ago. But what I've always remembered is when a group of young black boys needed help, instead of looking the other way …that older brother of a friend went back.

I'm a runner and one of the routes I run takes me by a convenience store. I usually go in and buy a bottle of water for the walk home. One night, a group of young black boys were inside, pooling their money to buy snacks. I stood behind them, knew they were short on change and smiled. "They're with me" I told the clerk. I did that because that older brother of a friend went back.

Years ago, I saw a little boy nervously fumbling around, trying to tie his tie before going into an interview. "I got you buddy", I told him. As I slowly tied that tie, I told him to be sure he looked that interviewer in the eyes and smile. Give a firm handshake and sit up straight and when they ask if you have any questions, ask them about their job – because one day you're going to be in that position. I did it because that older brother of a friend went back.

A few weeks ago. while in a coffee shop, I struck up a conversation with a young black boy. He asked me what I did, I told him I write. "Wow, that's so cool man!" I asked what he wanted to become, and he said a doctor. "That's even cooler" I shot back at him. We both laughed and before he bolted out, he told me he's a pole vaulter on his track team and invited me out to his meet. I already have my calendar cleared for that day… I did that because the older brother of a friend went back.

The world is filled with young black boys, looking for a man to speak for them in awkward situations, believe in their dreams and show up for them as they become realities. We just have to open our eyes – and hearts to see them. So, the next time you see one in need … don't just keep going, wondering what "that's" all about … because you never know who might be watching. You never know whose life might be changed because of your actions.

Go back … because that little black boy …

Is waiting on you …

Michael Wade

Losing a parent at any age is difficult, but it can be especially difficult for a small child. My siblings and I lost our mother when we were small and one of the things that I remember most is how our friends interacted with us following her passing. I can still see the expressions on their faces as they searched for the right things to say, the right ways to comfort. In most cases they didn't know what to say, so they just did. Some stopped by the house more, some saved seats on the school bus, some let us spend nights ... anything they could do to ease the hurt, they did. Through that pain bonds were strengthened and some of those friends became like family.

A few years back one of those friends lost his mother who just so happened to be one of mine's dearest friends. After her service, the neighborhood met at the family house for food, healing, and fellowship. I was one of the first people to arrive and grabbed a seat just off the side of the living room. Out of nowhere this friend appeared and pulled up a chair right next to mine. We made small talk touching on this, that after the other before taking a slight pause as I looked away and he did the same. I turned back only because he began patting me on my knee. He turned toward me, ***"Lynnie I didn't rest well for years after your mother passed man.*** I didn't rest well for years." I looked back at him but didn't say a word because his response answered any "why" I could've had. He said, "I just couldn't wrap my mind around the fact that someone who meant so much to all of us not being there any longer." He said it was only once he realized she was in a better place that he was able to rest...

This friend passed a few years back. and just like others who've gone before ... I miss him. Over the course of these last few years I saw him at a number of different outings. Each time he had the same warm, dignified way. The more I travel through life the more I've come to value qualities like those because they truly are hard to find. I miss that about him. Following his passing, I like so many others whose life he touched had a hard time wrapping our minds around him not being here. I had a hard time understanding that someone who meant so much to all of us was gone. But then one morning I stopped and thought about that conversation we had that day...and my heart smiled because I realized that from this point forward, he will always be in a better place...

Until our paths cross again ... rest easy friend ...

When Friends Become Family

When my old man moved out of the house we grew up in, I'll admit – it hit me hard. The day my brothers and I came over and packed him up, so many memories came to mind as I walked from room to room. I went out to the front porch, looked up and down the street and thought about all the good people...and all the good memories. Although he left that house, those memories of those good people that comprised that amazing neighborhood, will never leave me.

Texas summers are the worst. They're hot now but ask anyone who grew up in the 80's and 90's and they'll tell you the summers we have now pale in comparison to the ones we used to endure. We'd come out for brief periods during the day, but by the time I got to high school, my core group of friends spent most of our summers hanging out at night.

Ten o'clock was our official unofficial meeting time and for the next four or five hours – maybe longer, we hung. We'd throw footballs, dribble basketballs, have foot races, go to the corner store for "sweets" as my father often referred to the junk we'd buy. Those were some of the best times of my life.

The night, (morning) always had to end of course. Five of the guys lived right next door to one another while I lived a few houses down. I'd start my walk, look back and there was always this one friend who stood outside, looking at me as I made my way home. Night after night, I would turn around and there he was still looking.

Year after year, summer night after summer night, he did this. One night I asked why. He said he just wanted to make sure I got in the house safely. I assured him I had a key and I would be ok. ***He said he knew – he just wanted to be sure.*** Today, reach out to that friend. The one who even when everything said you were ok...stood watch and cared enough to make sure.

I love football ... but I was never big enough to play at a high level. I was tough enough, just not big enough – until the year after I graduated. The night I crossed the stage my senior year of high school I was 5'4 139 pounds. A year later – I was 5'9 195 pounds. The things I could've done in high school at that size...

I wasn't big enough, but I was determined to play. The first day of tryouts my freshman year, the freshman, junior varsity, and varsity teams worked out together. As the workout concluded, the time came for wind sprints and of course, I was the smallest one on the field. As we ran, all kinds of mocks and jeers came my way. He's too small...is he in the right grade...elementary school is down the street; I heard those and many others. More importantly, I heard the familiar voice of a good friend, much bigger than I and a couple grades older.

"Keep running Lynn...keep running man, you're doing fine. Don't listen to them...they can't break you man...you got this thing man!' I almost quit that day and I probably would have, no I would have had it not been for him, had it not been for his voice.

When things get tough, no matter the area of life they choose to get tough in, remember the familiar voice of that good friend. That good friend who when everyone else in life was saying you couldn't, believed in you enough to say you could.

My mother passed when I was a small child. As the years have gone by, other mothers from our neighborhood have been granted their wings. I remember attending the funeral of one of my mother's best friends – and a touching conversation I had with her son.

He said for years after my mother's passing, even as he went away to college, he had trouble sleeping. He said he just couldn't wrap his mind around how someone so special could be taken away from us like that.

Years later he was granted his wings, but as fate would have it, we took a picture together shortly before his passing. In that picture I was wearing my favorite blue shirt. As the years have gone by, it's come to mean so much more to me. Man, I love that shirt.

I don't send it to the cleaners, can't take no chances with that. I wash it, by hand. I wash it, by hand and each time I wear it, I think of that special friend. Man, I love that dude. Before walking out this morning, put on the love of a special someone who may have passed on, but left a special something for you to hold onto.

Remember the friend who stood watch...
Listen for the voice of the friend who said you could...
Never let go of the friends who've left...

They say blood is thicker than water, but it's a beautiful thing when water becomes blood...when friends become family.

Lynn's Flowers

Yellow cabs ... you don't see many on the road these days. I can't tell you the last time I rode in one ... but, I've had my fair share of rides in them. Yes, I got to know all about yellow cabs because my mother never learned how to drive. She simply had no interest so, on those days when my father wasn't around, she'd just call a trusty yellow cab.

Before calling, she'd get dressed, and boy could she dress. Made no difference where we were going ... that woman was always sharp. Accessorized just right, head adorned by a crown of silky black hair, wearing heels that were always just the right height. All this topped off by a sweet perfume touching you in a way that announced she was there, making you wish she'd never leave. That was my mother.

I can still hear her dignified voice saying, ***"yes, please send a cab to my home at 3107 Longview ...*** thank you ..." Shortly thereafter, that bright yellow cab would show up and off we went ... she and I against the day. Furniture stores, toy stores, doctor's offices, department stores ... if you can name it, chances are we made a stop there.

One trip in particular stands out. We had just finished another day of bonding as I've come to call those times we shared. She went over to the nearby pay phone and called a cab, signaling the end of our day. I stood peering into a store window, captivated by this beautiful bouquet of paper flowers. She came over, stood next to me, and asked if I liked them. I told her yes and with that she whisked me inside and purchased them.

Upon arriving home, we picked a spot for them, settling on my father's desk. For years after her passing, that bouquet of paper flowers sat there, a soft, yet powerful reminder of that beautiful day we spent together. Even though they couldn't be watered I made sure they never died. I wiped them down, dusted them off, and during dark days I looked to them for strength. Believe it or not, I even talked to them: yeah, I talked to paper flowers. They always talked back, in her voice.

Lynn's Flowers is what my father took to calling them. I moved away, but whenever I came home, from time to time at just the right time, he'd smile, look over at me before pointing to them and say, "there go your flowers Lynn ..."

Whenever I made a trip home, I always grabbed a room at my sisters, but first I'd stop by my fathers. During one stop as soon as I walked in, he tossed me a bag. This was nothing new as he always had a bag for me. A bag filled with my favorite chips, socks, underwear, toiletries – he always had a bag for me. "Open it" he said. I quickly untied the crude little knot and there were my flowers, all nice and cleaned up. "Put your flowers in your house" ... he said.

It wasn't Christmas, but it sure felt like it and I immediately started thinking about where in the house I would place them. On the fireplace mantle, my nightstand, the dining room table maybe. It didn't matter, all I knew is that I'd find a special place for those special flowers.

Time came for me to head back home, but before I did, I stopped by his place to say bye. We stood out on the porch as was our norm, talked for a few minutes before I began inching toward my car. He told me to be careful on that road and I promised I would. Just as I started to pull off, he motioned for me to roll my window down. He smiled and said, "remember your flowers …"

How could I forget my flowers?

The ones I couldn't water, but so many days they watered me. My flowers, the ones that spoke to me from the time we first laid eyes on one another and still speak to this very day. My beautiful flowers, reminders that even when a person departs, they'll always have a place in your heart. The light to my darkness is what those worn paper flowers have always been, making me smile when I should've frowned. Those beautiful flowers of mine they still hold a scent that announces she was here, making me wish she had never left … promising me, we'll see each other again.

Flowers don't always have stems, pretty petals, or heart-shaped leaves. A flower can be a compliment given many days ago, a person who believed in you when no one else did, a time you did when everything said you wouldn't. Those are flowers too. As you move through your day, through your life, challenges are bound to come in all shapes and sizes. When they do, when it seems as though the hope you held onto has come and gone …

Remember … your flowers.

The Little Black Boy Without a Voice

Whenever I find myself flipping through the channels, there are a few movies that I simply cannot bypass. It doesn't matter if I have something already set in my mind, when I see these I pause. One of them is the Shawshank Redemption, another is Good Will Hunting. But the one that forces me to drop the remote and tune out the world around me...is "Glory" starring Denzel Washington, Andre Braugher and Morgan Freeman.

One of my favorite scenes involves all three men and happens early on. The men of the 54th Massachusetts have been assigned their quarters and are bedding down for the night when out of nowhere comes a little black boy drumming loudly, making noise. Washington tired from a day of drills confronts the boy, telling him to go outside with all the noise but the boy doesn't respond. Instead he just stares. At this time Braugher informs him that the boy is a mute. Freeman looks back at him and says, "You mean this child can't talk?" Braugher firmly shakes his head no.

What Freeman, whose screen name was Major Rawlins, did next was powerful. Instead of turning and going off to sleep, he motions for the little boy to come to him and for the remainder of the movie wherever he went the little boy without a voice followed.

When he ate the little black boy without a voice was next to him. When he slept the little black boy without a voice lay beside him. When he trained the little black boy without a voice was off in a distance but watching. And before he fought what would be his final battle, the little black boy without a voice saw him off.

He guided him. ***He watched over him***. He provided an example for him. He stood and fought for him. He did all of this because Major Rawlins understood that the world can be a cruel place...for a little black boy...without a voice.

The world could use more men like Major Rawlins because there are still little black boys without voices. They find themselves in simple life situations with authorities that turn into complex conditions that lead to tragedies...because the little black boy is without a voice. They miss out on the life that should have been and settle for the one they have...because they can't speak the language. They land behind bars, they're shot dead in the streets, their dreams go unfulfilled...because no one ever spoke for them.

If you happen upon one, drumming loudly...making noise don't send him away, pull him close. Guide him...watch over him...be the example he can follow and above all stand and fight for him... Fight with honor, it'll show that little black boy what it means to be a man. Watch him watch you

– then watch how much more conscious you become in who you are becoming. Above all know that child is staring because he can't talk but he's dying to be heard, so talk for him.

Because the world can be a cruel place...for a little black boy...

Without a voice...

Everybody Loves Raymon

I like television. I don't watch it nearly as much as I used to, but the television is still a part of my life. When it comes to movies, if you can give me a good period piece, I'm all yours. A documentary will hold my attention for hours and if you can point me in the direction of any football game, you've made a friend for life. But while all these categories are good, nothing captures my attention more than what I call, simple television.

Simple television like Frasier, Cheers, Girlfriends and my one of my new favorites – Everybody Loves Raymond! The show ended way back in 2005, but you can still catch reruns and catch them I do. The show centers on Raymond – a sportswriter and all-around good guy and his incredibly challenging, yet hilarious relationship with his family.

From his father who often acts like a bratty little kid to his quick-witted mother who wears the pants in the family to his boorish big brother who takes great pride in getting on Raymond's nerves, the show is a hoot. The show is a hoot and for me, it offers a welcome escape.

The end of each show finds Raymond and his wife Debra, lying in bed, discussing their day before both drift off to sleep. I always believe it's at this point, no matter what the day has brought, challenges, victories, defeats or somewhere in between, the central character realizes...that through it all...

Everybody loves Raymond...

I was talking to a friend last week via email. We went back and forth a few times before finally reaching a conclusion. The last thing he said was, "praying for your pops." I got a text from another one of the fellas a few nights ago, out of the blue. He wasn't asking about my tournament bracket (which by the way, is in shambles), he said nothing about shooting pool or hanging out. His text said, "Checking in on the old man LP ..."

Former co-workers who've now become close friends have called here of late. We laugh till we cry, discussing all the crazy people we worked with and even crazier things we did while working with them. Special conversations they are – they become even more special when they pause and in a very authentic voice tell me their thoughts are with my dad.

My brother went down to see him a few weeks ago. The rehab facility he was housed in has a four-hour window that allows residents to leave the premises. So, he scooped him up, put him in his truck and took him for a spin. When my father called, he sounded like a little kid at the playground, swinging on a swing. He was happy to be out of the facility no doubt – but I think, nah, *I know he was happier just because he was hanging out with his son.*

My father's first name is Raymon – Raymon with no "d" as his doctors love to say. Those same doctors are also quick to remind him that he has cancer. True to his character (you'd have to be in the room when he says this) he's just as quick to tell them, "if I got cancer…I can't tell!"

Every time I speak with him, he has one of his silly jokes that crack him and only him up. "Squirrels are looking for you man – they think you're a nut …" Yeah, he kills himself with those types of corny one-liners.

He doesn't feel it, but they assure him, it's there all the same. Here of late, they took him off medication. But the prayers, the texts, the well wishes, visits and thoughts from friends and family, near and far away keep coming in. That's the medication he's on these day … it's working quite well. The doctors don't quite understand it, they never have, but it's simple. He keeps getting up, smiling, laughing, and living one day at a time because through it all, he's come to realize…

That everybody loves Raymon…

Carrie

When I was in college, I dreamed of being that corporate guy … you know the who spends all day wheeling, dealing, and leading from the office perfectly situated for all to see! I held onto that dream and upon graduating, I hit the job market seeking to make it a reality, but life … had other ideas. I applied and applied, went on God knows how many interviews, but I just couldn't close the deal – until I finally did!

That's right a door finally opened and although it was only an entry-level opportunity, an opportunity was all I ever wanted. I got there with big ideas, filled with ambition, and focused on making up for lost time. But there was one problem – I was assigned to work for a manager who worked against me. It didn't matter what I did – stay late, come early, volunteer, or go every extra mile, there was nothing I could do to get him in my corner. Making matters worse was the fact he created a false narrative, telling everyone -- including the Director that I was a poor performer, knowing full well nothing could be further from the truth. Well, as fate would have it, he was eventually terminated, ironically enough for his poor performance. His dismissal meant a new lease on my corporate life … and a new manager. This manager was nothing like the first one. She was fair, balanced, kind and most important of all, *she believed in me.*

Around this same time, I began receiving emails from a female member of the diversity team geared toward women in IT. She and I had never met and just like so many others, she assumed based on the spelling of my first name that I was a female. Happened (and still happens!) all the time. No worries I thought, I'll just blow it off as always. Well, one afternoon after receiving yet another one of those emails, I decided the time had come to kill the awkwardness. With that, I sent her a very polite note telling her that I was in fact … a man. Turns out she was actually in my building and felt so embarrassed by the mix-up she invited me down to meet. We had a good laugh and before leaving she agreed to become my career mentor, something I desperately needed in this new corporate terrain I was desperately trying to navigate.

Shortly thereafter she found herself dealing with a family emergency that called for her to move across the country. Before she could she had to find someone to fill her position – so she called me. We discussed her situation, the position, and how we'd go about grooming me. After a few weeks, we both knew I still needed work, but we figured I'd make up what I lacked in knowledge through effort.

Things were moving fast – I mean really fast and the next step was interviewing with her California-based manager. Our first conversation was via phone at which time she told me the interview process entailed three steps before a final decision would be made. The first was to be a phone interview, but as fate would have it, she would be in my city the following week and asked for a personal meeting to which I hurriedly agreed. We met and about 10 minutes in she abruptly stopped and said, "I know what I see across from me and I'm going to go ahead and extend an offer …" I accepted of course but walked out in a daze … but excited! The next day I told my manager and transfer and start dates for my new position were set. Once I left that organization, that's when I began understanding that the entire experience was a move of God.

You see, I later found out the Director had already put the wheels in motion for my termination telling managers on her staff including my new one that I was to be, "worked out of her organization" … even after she saw my performance. But while Director had set her wheels in motion, God had already started His. Turns out my new manager specifically asked that I begin reporting to her. When I arrived, she listened to me, guided me, she saw and believed in – that was God moving.

The emails from the female in IT and me finally responding to them; that was God moving. The fact that she was in my building, my building out of all of the others the company owned on the day I responded -- was God moving. The hiring manager being in my city and interviewing me in person instead of on the phone -- was God moving because what she saw in person triggering the job offer, couldn't have been seen over the phone.

But here's the one that always gets me. In order to get the new position, in order to get to the point where the move was made…the Director who thought so lowly of me had to approve it…but it passed right by her. I later found out that after I left, she asked, "How did this happen? My decision was to have him worked out of our organization!" My new manager and I laughed and figured God heard her decision and agreed with it -- He just took it a step further.

I never became the corporate guy I thought I'd be when I arrived. I never wheeled, "dealed" and I never got that office. In fact, I ended up officing out of my home. Go figure. But I learned that no matter how hard you try or how good your best is … It'll never be good enough for some people. Most of all, I learned that what God has for you is for you and as long as there are good people in the world, nothing and no one can stop it.

Shhhh!

The Book of Daniel is one of the more interesting in the Bible as it follows the life of this incredible man of God. Through it, we learn of Daniel's unending faith and the role in played in his surviving several life challenges, most notably the dreaded lion's den.

This book also speaks of his incredible ability to interpret visions and dreams; unmatched by any of his contemporaries, allowing him to curry favor with King Nebuchadnezzar. The final chapter sees Daniel receiving a vision unlike any he'd seen before, only this time he was cautioned not to share it. Instead, he's told to seal up the book holding that vision until the end of time.

Bible scholars have debated for centuries as to why Daniel was told to close the book with each having rational answers that seem valid. I myself once posed this question to a preacher during a Bible study some years back. Her answer...has stayed with me. She said Daniel was told to seal up the book that held the visions, because if he told those around him what was to come...***they simply wouldn't have been able to handle it...***

A lot of us share our visions for this reason or that one. It might be for validation, conversation, or any number of causes, but in most cases, we're wide open with these things. That's not always the best idea. That's not always the best idea, because sometimes we're given a vision that isn't to be shared. Those, "seal up the book" moments take wisdom to recognize. It takes wisdom to know when God is speaking to you and even more wisdom to know the vision you get from those conversations...aren't to be shared. Don't share them, because in many cases the persons you share them with are placed in your path to be nothing more than dream breakers and stealers.

So, the next time God comes to you with a vision, a dream, or a direction He is about to take you, keep it to yourself; that's right...seal it up. You'll feel guilty or maybe awkward but don't stay there long. Truth is friend for what God is about to do for you and the places He is about to take you if you told those dream breakers and dream stealers...

They simply wouldn't be able to handle it...

This ... Person

I know this person. We're not particularly close although we've known each other for quite some time. They're the kind who went out searching for the next big thing in a bad way. Beer was the next big thing...but never big enough. Wine was the next big thing...but never big enough. Marijuana was the next big thing...but never big enough...and since those things were never big enough, this person went onto other things...but they were never big enough.

One high begat another high; one addiction begat another addiction until those highs and addictions became the worst possible things they could become; habits...destructive habits that wreaked havoc. From a distance I prayed and from what I've been told, others did the same. Finally, that person began praying. Well, as it turns out, God heard those prayers, all of them and this person ... was delivered. He went in, took them by the hand, led them out of this dark room and closed that door.

You should've seen them after they walked through it. They had a beaming smile, they had pep in their step, and kind words always flowed from their mouth...this person actually glowed. This person still had the key so a couple of years ago they checked the lock on that closed door and found out it still worked so they opened it. Because it opened, they poked their head in to have a look around. Thinking they were strong enough, so they went ahead and walked all the way in...big mistake.

I saw this person not too long ago and sadly...I barely recognized them. That beaming smile was now a frown. That pep that they had in their step has been replaced by erratic life patterns that sees them sleep the day away so they can be ready to chase the night. Kind words turned hateful and the glow they once had has turned into a dark and ugly cloud. All this happened because that person dared to go back through that closed door. How did this happen if He closed it you ask? Well here's the thing...He closes the door but, in many cases just like this person, you and I still want to hold onto the key.

At certain points in all of our lives we'll be tempted to place the key in the lock of a closed door and walk back through it. Might be a closed door to a relationship, might be a thing or it might be a place because doors come in all types of situations and circumstances. But remember, if He closes a door, He closed it for a reason… and just because the key still fits in the lock and the door opens…that doesn't necessarily mean it was meant for you to walk back through it.

When He closes a door, pray that He locks it…but more importantly, pray that God gives you the strength to throw away the key…

I'm an Explorer

I grew up in the 70's and 80's and if the gray around my temples didn't give me away, my choice of slang would. From time to time slang from that period will just roll out of my mouth so free and fluid that it's almost like I was still living in that period. Someone will ask if I've seen so and so. My response will be something along the lines of "yeah I ran into that cat a few months back…." (cat refers to a friend or associate).

On another occasion a friend might ask how things are on my end, my response will almost surely have the word cool in it somewhere. (cool means everything is just fine). My favorite 70's slang saying of all time would be…selling wolf tickets. A friend might be hurling insults and threats at another and I will say something like, "be cool man; that cat's just selling a bunch of wolf tickets … "

A few years back, I bumped into an old head (older cat) at the gym and we struck up a conversation…and the slang started rolling. The NBA playoffs were in full swing and come to find out he actually went to grade school with one of the competing coaches. He said way back in the day when they was running the yards (playgrounds) in Chi (Chi meaning Chicago), every time he pulled up to take a J (jump shot) it was automatic systematic (the shot always went in). He was around about 6'5 and said every time one of those turkeys (someone who couldn't play well) brought some jive (a bad shot) into the lane he'd block it and tell them to, "Stop bringing that Kool-Aid to my Malt Liquor party …" (please make a better decision)…

A couple of days later our paths crossed again. I was sitting in the gym locker room rummaging through my bag and heard his voice. "What's happening young blood (directed at a person younger than you asking how their day is going)…It had been a long day and in keeping with the little slang vibe that we had going, I looked up and smiled and said, "I'm a survivor …" Contrary to popular belief, "I'm a survivor" is a phrase that was around long before Destiny's Child and means that no matter what life throws at you, you're going to make it.

He laughed heartily and shot back at me saying, "oh you a survivor huh?" I laughed too and said, "dig." We broke from 70's mode for a minute and he said, "my man, being a survivor ain't good enough." He smiled and tilted his head in a way that said, "now dig this" before saying, "I'm an explorer…because I'm the type who wants to go out there and find out what all this bleeding, sweating, and surviving was all about. *I'm an explorer young blood … and that's what I want you to be.*"

How many times have you survived something only to be content...that you actually survived? The real blessing of surviving is having the strength, courage and faith that come from being willing to go and find out what it was that you were surviving to see. That's what explorers do.

Make it a point to stop being content with just making it from day to day or year to year, surviving. Make up your mind to change, because when you do that's when you go from simply existing to truly living. That's when you make the transition from being just a survivor to actually becoming...an explorer!

Right on? Right on!

Northstar

So, I grew up on Longview Drive...bought my first house on Watch Hill Court...and I moved...to Northstar Drive. Every time I turn that corner, no matter if I'm driving, running, or walking, I can't help but think how fitting it is that I'd end up here. Fitting because in my life – the North Star has played such a pivotal role.

She's always been my guide.

Mothers are often referred to as the North Star because they shine brightest when a child's in need of direction, guidance, love, and support. I heard this a long time ago and I believe it now, even more strongly than I did in years past. I have an old friend and his mother used to always commend my father for remaining with me and my siblings after my mother passed. In the 1970's it was commonplace for a widower to place his children under the care of a sister, an aunt or a mother...but ours didn't do that.

He chose to stick it out.

He chose to stick it out and that beautiful lady would commend him and take time to commend me as well because she knew the struggles a child faced without a mother. She once told me, "you can have a million fathers but without your mother, the world can be a tough place, so I'm here for you whenever you need me son." Anyone who has experienced this knows what I mean. Years later, she passed and since that time this friend and I along with a few others have developed an even deeper bond because we now share this indescribably beautiful pain.

I like stars, always have, and suspect I always will. What I like best about stars, especially the North Star; especially mine is that she shines brightest in our lives during the cloudiest of seasons. Not in our eyes but in our hearts. Seems like yesterday but she left for a better place over 40 years ago. Forty years ago, but I can still hear her voice saying turn this way or that way boy, feel her touch telling me when to stop and when to go. Feel her sitting next to me when no one else is willing or wants to.

Life is hard with seasons that are wrought with challenges that seemingly go on forever. But it gets easier if you refuse to quit. Oh, you'll want to, but on those days when you feel as though quitting time has come and you can't go on... look to your North Star...the one who never quit on you.

When life gets cloudy and you can't find your way...look to your North Star...because even the clouds, the stormiest of days can't cover her. If things go dark, and they will, and you lose sight of who you are, and you will, look to your North Star...because she'll never forget.

There will be others in the sky, but she'll be easy to spot.

She'll be the one shining the brightest because her child's in need of direction...guidance...love, and support...

The Runner

Slavery was an institution wrought with evil, sadistic customs, one of which...was labeling. Masters and Overseers had a slew of labels for slaves that in effect told the world how to regard them. There was the label "Hot Tail", given to that young female slave(s) in most cases by the master's wife out of hatred due to the fact that she (the "Hot Tail") was engaged in sexual relations with several men on the plantation, most notably...the master. Never mind the fact that these relations were forced upon her, in some cases for breeding and in others as a mechanism of control...she was labeled.

When it came to the male slave, "Boy" was the word of choice. At a certain age, any eye can make the distinction between a boy and a man but in the eyes of the slave master, there was none; every male slave...was called "Boy." This was strategic and purposed as slave masters recognized more than the male slave himself, more than that man, more than that "Boy" that percolating just below that docile black countenance was the ever so subtle yet fierce reminder that he was meant to be a king. Slave masters worked tirelessly to eradicate this...hence, the use of the label, "Boy."

But there was one label that made every slave master tremble with fear by day and had every overseer standing at their post by night. That label...was "Runner." No, this slave wasn't working out, running laps around the plantation. Oh no, the "Runner" was that brave soul who dared to think outside of those walls that held his body but not his mind, setting his sights on living the life that was destined for him, without chains.

Slave masters hated the "Runner" ... because he just didn't get it. They hated him with a passion because they knew he was brave. Catch him the first time and give him 39 lashes on his bare back...no problem, he'll just heal up and in 5 months or so, try again. Catch him the second time and chop off one his big toes, no worry master...he'll wait until that maiming gets better, set out with 9 toes, and use the lessons learned to go even further.

Catch him that third time...not happening. Not happening because, by this time, the "Runner" has tasted what being free feels like. He has tasted freedom and even with a forever scarred back and a foot that will never again be complete, he understands that a cage is no longer fit for him.

Slave masters hated the "Runner" with a passion but not just for his propensity to run but because if the truth is told, the "Runner" was actually a "Messenger", telling others who were bound there was something better. After being caught the first time, when he was skinned by the lash, he may have fainted from the loss of blood but the fire in his eyes never went out and it caused flames, young flames to start flickering.

After having his toe removed, his brother, his sister allowed him to lean on them during recovery and all the while he whispered in their ear, ***"Look at what we can do, together."*** And when he finally broke free on that third time, in many cases never to see their faces again, his lasting message was simple yet powerful and said...If I can do it...so...can...you...

Someone is watching you today, waiting to see if you are going to be a "Runner", waiting for, yearning for the message you bring. It might be your son, it might be your daughter, hey it might be the kid a few streets over with no father of his own who is ever so close to falling in with the wrong crowd.

They're watching to see if the fire still burns in your eyes after the first attempt and failure...don't let it go out; it's what will start theirs. They're watching to see who you hang with, who you roll with when you make your second attempt...choose wisely and they will too.

More importantly, they're watching to see the day you finally break free because when you do, him, her, they, mine, yours, theirs, whoever...will come to realize that because you did it...

So...can...they...

The Lesson of the Clouds

I started watching the clouds as a little boy. Sometimes alone and then other times with friends as we raced and embraced the innocence of life as only small children growing up in a small town could. It was never planned; it just happened and each time it did, there we stood looking up, eagerly pointing out this shape or the next.

One friend might say he saw a fire engine with a long ladder hanging off to the side. Yet another would claim he saw a Corvette, with big tires ready to eat up the road as burning rubber would not be a fair depiction. Another friend would swear up and down...he saw Superman himself, cape, and all, standing there, prepared to come down and protect us from any amount of harm.

Later on, as I briefed my mother on my day, I would tell her everything I saw when I looked up. I would tell her about the dog, the motorcycle, the castle, and the horses. Each time I told her she would sit there smiling, lovingly soaking it all in.

The lesson of the clouds is what she called it as we looked up and talked to the clouds, through our small eyes, minds, and hearts. ***And the most beautiful part of it all...is*** that the clouds talked back ...

I still find myself doing this from time to time. It might come at the end of a long run or happen at the end of a long day. I see all of those shapes and characters but only now, I see so much more. Some days I see love then others, strength, hope, and courage but I never walk away without getting something. That's the lesson of the clouds my mother spoke so fondly of.

Friend the next time you're feeling down...look up at the clouds because they hold a lesson; they really do. More importantly, they hold a blessing. Look up and talk to them with your eyes, your mind, and your heart, because when you do something beautiful happens...

The clouds talk back...

So glad I took that call

I moved to Arlington, Texas way back in 1989 and while it seems like yesterday, that was over 30 years ago. Arlington was not my first choice as I had originally made plans to go elsewhere, but when my financial aid package was declined, those plans went by the wayside. When I arrived, I set my sights on UT-Arlington, but even though I had a new school I had the same old problem: finances.

Back then temporary agencies were everywhere with offers of short and long-term work assignments, so I signed on with a few to make some fast money. They kept me working, but it seemed every single time I got into a financial groove, the assignment would end, and I'd find myself right back at square one: financially strapped with no way to pay for school. To make matters worse, one assignment ended due to an injured shoulder – the last thing I needed. The injury forced me to wear a cumbersome harness but more importantly, it forced me to miss work – something a guy like me who was trying to fund a college education couldn't afford. Time was of the essence as a new semester was staring me straight in the face and unfortunately, I had no answers.

Out of nowhere one of the agencies called with another assignment and my sister, even though she could sense I wasn't in the mood to talk, passed me the phone. I started to just hang it up, but I didn't, and by the end of the call I was working … at least temporarily. Even though I was injured, I was working and set to start that following Monday.

So, Monday rolled around, and after a long weekend of thinking, I had made up my mind that I wasn't going in, but I went in anyway…and kept going in…and kept going in…until one afternoon the boss called me into his office. I figured this was the dreaded "your assignment has ended conversation"; but boy was I wrong. Instead he said, "I've asked the temporary agency for permission to hire you permanently" …the words every temp worker wants to hear. So, in a space of 15 minutes, I went from making $5.15 per hour…to $45,000 a year; at 20 years of age. Financial problems…tuition, rent, car, books…all those problems and more…instantly solved.

I often wonder what my life would've been like had I not shown up for work that first Monday, but I'm so grateful that I did. I stayed at that job for 10 years, bought 3 new cars, traveled, completed my undergraduate degree, and began working on my MBA. I made lifelong friends and in effect, I went from a boy to a man.

The irony of it all came rushing back to me on my last day as God spoke to me in several ways. First, He spoke through a mirror. I visited my old workstation, the very first one I had and for some reason there was a mirror there, sitting boldly, beckoning for me to come closer. I did and when

I looked in it, I saw a man with a moustache and a stubbled beard looking back at me, nothing like the boy who arrived without a hair on his clean, just out of teens face.

He next spoke to me through silence. As I walked through the plant one final time there wasn't a soul around as everyone else had left early but by this time, I had transferred to a department that worked late. The lights were dimmed, the machines were off and there wasn't a sound to be heard. It made me stop and think about how much noise my life held when I arrived...noise that said don't go Monday, noise that said you're injured, noise that said you're running out of time. But in that moment of silence, I remembered how He quieted all that noise down and led me to a place that offered me peace.

The last and most powerful way was through a simple calendar. I walked past the inspection area where I also worked once and saw one sitting on the table. It said August 14th, 1999... I was hired permanently on August 14th, 1989. My first day and last day fell on the same date. I've held onto those conversations, those reminders, those remember Me's, those it's going to be ok's and every so often, I lean on them. But none of them would've ever happened had I not taken the call, or had I decided not to go in that Monday.

Take it from me -- when things get tight take the call and above all no matter how much noise you hear that says not to, says stay away, says it won't work, go in anyway...

Because going in...is where your blessing can be found.

N-word

I used to be a day runner but with my schedule becoming busier, the vast majority of my runs are now done at night. Tonight, I have the night off but there have been times I have laced up my shoes and set out, chasing that goal of completing a marathon this coming December at 11 PM; sometimes later.   I know; it sounds crazy right but hey, you got to do what you got to do sometimes, right?

I've been running around this area for so long that I can just about tell you the distance from my house to anywhere within a 15-20-mile radius. The 7-11 at the end of the street, that's 1.3 miles, my friend. That CVS Pharmacy that closes at midnight, 2.1 miles with a decline if you're heading north and an incline if you're heading south. It's 6.3 miles to the mall, an even 2 miles to the Neighborhood Walmart and just a shade over 3 miles to reach the post office. Yep, I know them all and then some like the back of my hand.

During the days when I run, you ought to see me as a large part of the workout is spent waving. A honk here, someone shouting my first name there, a point or nod of the head, I get them all. Yes, I guess you could say I'm a regular on the road and honestly, I have no problem with that; none whatsoever. But most of my runs...take place at night.

Four things happen to me when I run at night. First, I sweat...a lot. Second, I get tired because, by the time I take off I've worked a full day and dealt with my share of challenges. The third thing I can count on...is a good night rest. Oh yes, you get out there and run 5, 6, 8, 9 miles or more and rest assured, you're going to sleep well. The fourth thing I can count on is...a little different.

Nearly every time I run at night, no matter the route or distance, a car, a truck, an SUV...will zoom by me...and scream the word no black man, woman, or child wants to hear...

"Nigger ...."

It happened three times last night I guess you could say they were on a roll. The first time a group pulled up close and yelled, "Go home nigger." The second time, a truck stopped, and the passenger used his hands as a fake machine gun, made the shooting sound and said, "Die Nigger die...." The last one saw a car filled with men (I use that term loosely). The driver said," roll Call...roll Call...Nigger...Nigger!"

The ones calling me that name...they look nothing like me. They never stop...I wish they would, I really do.
The irony of it all is that I'm sure some of these same people probably pass me by on those mornings, those days when I'm running, honk a horn, smile, and wave. But at night, under the cover of darkness...things change.

They say that ugly word in the dark but here's my problem...they might be the one making a hiring decision in the light. They use the cover of night to say that word but when the sun rises, they might be the cop looking to make a name for himself. They say that name during the pitch black dark of night but when the gorgeous sun rises, they could be sitting behind a desk at a bank, deciding if someone who looks like me gets approved for the loan that will unlock their future.

It pains me to see how so many people assume that since we had a Black president since we are no longer in chains, since our schools have long been integrated...racism no longer exists. Nothing could be further from the truth.

For those of you who think racism no longer exists, I (and some of my brothers and sisters) could tell you a far different tale. Don't believe us...watch for yourself. Watch how the crowd subtly shifts to the other side...when a black man gets on the elevator. Hey, listen to the doors lock when a black man or woman walks through a crowded walkway...in broad daylight. Observe and listen when a young black boy or girl is articulate...and how their teacher marvels at this feat...like the young black boy or girl were never supposed to be able to speak.

It's important that the name that I get called on the regular be kept in the light...even though it's done in the dark. Expose I say, show them for who they truly are...that's the only way true healing can begin.

I know you're wondering...where does this atrocity occur time and time again...where oh where do I live you ask...

I live in the United States of America...

Just...like...you...

Run

Running is a strange addiction; ***you love it and you hate it***, sometime at the same time. There are those days when you awaken and can't wait to get out on the road and see where it takes you. Then there are those other days when you simply dread lacing up your running shoes. You dread it with a passion man, you self-complain and pout...but in the midst of it all, you know you'll get it done; you know you'll answer the pavement's call.

Every runner has their story of how they came to be a road warrior. My story centers on my father, his centers on my mother. It seems like yesterday, but she passed well over 40 years ago and in her wake, she left quite the challenge. Six children to raise, a household to run, bills to pay...yes indeed he was up against it. All these things were challenges, but the greatest one he faced ... was time. Yes, time was his enemy and the more time he had on his hands, the more time he had to think about who and what he lost.

To keep from thinking about it, he got three jobs and he'd shuttle from this job to the next with little or no time in between. He worked as many hours as he possibly could and then one day...he ran out of hours and came face to face with time. There were no more jobs to go to, no more shifts to work, no place to hide. Out of his mind with grief, he took off running right where he was...in a button-down shirt, slacks, and wingtips.

He didn't go far, but as he ran, he noticed how good it felt. On the walk back to his car he decided to try it again the next day, this time in proper attire. He kept going day after day and each time he noticed how much better he felt, how much clearer he thought, how much stronger physically, emotionally, and mentally he became. My father ran until he passed because, in his words, "I had someplace to go and God knew standing still wasn't going to get me there...so He sent me off running ..."

There's something you're facing, have been facing for quite some time. You look at it and it looks back at you but it...whatever it is, wasn't sent here to go anywhere. You on the other hand...you were. The biggest mistake you can make is to continue to stand still, hiding, hoping, and wishing it away. Whether it's personal or professional, no matter what facet of life the challenge may reside...it's time to go. God has something amazing planned for you, but you've got to stop standing still... And start running...

Are you cold?

I started running because my father was and still is a runner. Hey, I guess it gives credence to that old adage like father, like son. As a child our runs always took place during the early morning hours which is great if you're trying to avoid the brutal Texas heat. During the winter, leaving early was a bit of a problem because contrary to popular belief...the winters in Texas can be harsh.

On those winter mornings, we would start off slow, blowing smoke as our warm inside met the cold outside. The conversation would center on school, home, this, or that and all of a sudden, he'd look down and ask, "Are you cold?" My response would almost always be yes. His response was to ***keep moving.***

We would go a little further and the conversation would go a little deeper. Seeds were being planted, lessons were being taught and a man was being made. "How's school ... tell me about this little friend...who was that calling the house the other night...?" Then out of nowhere,

"Are you still cold?"

"A little."

"We need to turn back?"

"No."

"Good, let's keep going ..."

Let's keep going, yes, let's keep going. The run would take us down this street and that one, by friend's homes, by still closed businesses and those that in the early hours had already opened their doors. "You talk to any of your brothers here lately...call them this week...what are they paying you on that little job you got now...don't spend it all in one place now...

"You cold ...?"

"Nah; I'm good ..."

I smiled, he smiled back.

I'm a lot like you. I've been in some cold places that had absolutely nothing to do with the weather. Some of you are cold now but before turning back, remember those early morning runs life called you to take.

The layoff at the job made things cold but you kept going, you warmed up. Someone left but you warmed up only because you kept moving. Things fell apart in every sense of the phrase, but you got warm again, you didn't stop, you kept moving...

So, when life asks if you're cold, even when you are, or if you want to turn back, keep going. Remember those runs, the lessons you learned, the seeds that were harvested and the person that you fought so hard to become. Listen closely and you'll hear life ask, "you cold?"

When it does...smile big and say, "Nah; I'm good ..."

And watch life smile back at you....

Next

One of the things I miss so much from my days growing up in Killeen, Texas is being able to run across the street to the park for a game of pickup basketball. It didn't matter what time of the year, there was always someone hooping at "the courts" as that part of our neighborhood came to be called. It could be the dead of winter complete with cold, biting winds in your face or the heart of the summer with heat mercilessly bearing down on the asphalt. It didn't matter as there was always someone at the courts.

The daily routine was simple. It'd start out with one or two persons showing up with a ball, hoisting up jumpers, practicing their favorite moves or trying out that impossible dunk. The pounding of the ball on the pavement was like a call to action for all those within earshot and once it was heard it was dutifully obeyed.

Before you knew it, the courts were teeming with guys from all over the neighborhood. Then like clockwork, someone would utter a familiar four-word phrase, "Let's run a game!" It didn't matter whose mouth it rolled out of, time always stood still and before our very eyes, an innocent playground would transform into a battlefield.

Young men of all ages would line up at the free throw line, vying to become team captain which ultimately secured them a spot on the court. The first two persons to sink a free throw were anointed and given the right to choose their teams and this, my friend, is where the strategy came into play.

You might love his mama's chocolate cake...but was he going to give you the best chance to win? His sister is best friends with the girl you have a crush on, but can he play ball? He stood up to that bully for you in the 3rd grade...but he hasn't hit a shot since the 3rd grade...all of that came into play.

Teams were chosen, and the lucky ones stretched and got in a couple last minute practice jumpers before the game started. Those that weren't chosen called what was known as "next" meaning when the game was over, they would be a captain and have the chance to pick a team to challenge the winners.

If you chose the right teammates...you could be on the court winning and having fun all day. If you chose the wrong teammates...you might find yourself off to the side waiting and spectating and thinking about what could have been...hoping one of those guys that hollered next would pick you up for another run...

The more I think about all those days up there at the courts the more I've come to realize that the basketball games played there turned out to be the perfect metaphor for the game of life. Success on those courts started with the teammates that were chosen...and success in life follows that same path.

If you chose the right teammates, you'd be out there on those courts winning all day...by the same token if you chose the right teammates in life...you'll be out there on those courts too...winning...all day...

Choose your teammates wisely and align yourself with people who share your ideals. You're the captain of this team so be sure to only go with the people that empower and help you reach your goal of winning in this game. Don't waste your time on people who don't because you only got this one life...so be careful with your choices.

Because you don't get a next...

Me and my Shadow

Covering a song or doing a remake as its most commonly referred to, has been around almost as long as the music industry itself. Over the years, some of our most beloved listens have actually been covers; remade by a different artist looking to add a layer to the original. A guitar here, a piano riff there, a beat or two, a voice inflected this way or that way – anything to make something old seem new.

If one were to rank songs by the number of times they were remade, "Me and my Shadow" would be at or near the top. Written by Al Jolson, Dave Dreyer and Billy Rose, the song debuted in 1927 and was an immediate hit. Over the years it's been remade by a veritable who's who of entertainers. From Frank Sinatra to Bing Crosby to Sammy Davis Jr., Lou Rawls, and Pearl Bailey, some of our greatest talents have heeded the call of this alluring track.

It's a playful tune and no matter the voice, it's always sung with a smile, but if you listen closely you can't help but sense a tinge of sorrow. It speaks of daily travels and travails, loneliness, and despair. The voice looks for companionship, someone to comfort and support them along the way but … the only presence felt … is the shadow. There are touches of hope, but the song ends darkly, but even in the darkness, the presence of the shadow shines bright.

"Here comes your shadow" is what my father used to say to my mother each time she moved. That was his way of playfully alerting her that their youngest child was hot on her tail. That's right, from the time I was able to walk, if my mother moved … so did I. In a true motherly fashion, she carried me at first. A tiny woman, her friends used to marvel at her standing for what seemed like forever, me wrapped so tightly around her hip that you couldn't tell where I began, and she ended.

When I started walking, I promise you she never left my sight. If she was hanging sheets on the clothesline, I was there getting lost in them. If mom was in the kitchen preparing dinner, I was by her side. When the family gathered to watch television, there was no need to save me a seat – her lap was my seat and it goes without saying it was the best one in the house. If she moved … her shadow moved with her.

Three short months after my seventh birthday, I was there, but my mother was gone. The angels came calling saying something about needing her back and well … we all know how beautifully those conversations end. And when it ended, it was just me. Before the angels called him, my father and I would have the best conversations about her. During those times he'd glow with the light of her love and it warmed my heart to see it happen.

Those were some of our best times and I always dug deep, exploring him to find parts of her I never found when she was here. And the more we talked, the more her he found in me. "That's your mama talking right there … you get that from Lamona … oh yeah, that ain't none of me— that's her …" is what he used to say whenever he saw her rise up in me.

During one of those conversations I got it, I figured it all out and it comforted me in ways words can't describe. The moment the angels came for her and I ceased in being her shadow … was the same moment they sent her back and she became mine. When life was good, and I thought it was just me … it wasn't. In the darkest hours, the ones where I made it to light not knowing how I did and came out thinking it was just me … it wasn't. At all points of life, good, bad, and in between, when I thought it was just me, I'm comforted to know … it wasn't …

It was me … and my shadow …

Peace is Waiting on you

To get a dog … or to not get a dog, or two … that is the question I ponder at least once (actually more than that), a week. I'm sure at some point I'll give in to the urge of welcoming a furry companion to the house. While I don't have dogs of my own, they've become a big part of my life and through them, I've learned some valuable life lessons.

My father … all 90-something years of him owns an enormous pit bull named Texas. Texas has to weigh close to 80 pounds – maybe more with a bark that's bigger than she is. Whenever you ring his doorbell, her voice is the first one you hear. Next comes her menacing face, growling, snarling, barking, peering through the glass front door. It's the most unwelcoming welcome you could ever imagine.

In years past, he'd usher Texas to the back whenever I'd come by, well aware of my distrust of that particular breed. With his health declining to the point where he can no longer walk her to the back, Texas began staying in the room with us … growling, snarling with that ever-present stare.

One afternoon as he and I … and Texas, sat there talking, I took a chance. I kneeled down and held my hand out toward Texas, beckoning for her to come to me … confused she took a few steps before finally coming within my reach. I began patting her on the head. About a minute later, I softly tapped her cheeks at which time she smiled as only a dog can. Before long, she had rolled over on her back, eyes closed as I rubbed her stomach. In a span of about 5 minutes, this monster of a dog had melted right before my very eyes.

Nowadays whenever I come home, it's a different story. Texas still peers through the glass door only now, she runs back and forth like an anxious puppy, unable to contain the excitement she feels from seeing me. There's no more barking, only soft whimpers of joy. She no longer stands at a distance, she plops right down beside me and for however long I'm there… Texas and I, are inseparable.

I laughed with my father and told him all these years Texas and I have been frowning at each other, archenemies and now, we're at peace". He smiled back and says, "She was just waiting on you" …

There's something in your life that you've been putting off facing out of fear or distrust of what it might do to you. A person, a place, a call you've been delaying or a matter that's been on your mind. Chances are, it's nowhere near as bad as you think it is so today, take a moment, take a chance, reach out and deal with it.

The peace you've been seeking ... is waiting on you ...

High Blood Pressure

For the longest time, I hadn't been feeling like myself and it really began to bug me. In my younger days I'd be up at the crack of dawn, after falling asleep – at the crack of dawn. It didn't matter I was still filled with enough energy to function, be productive and do whatever needed to be done with no challenges whatsoever. Those days are long gone and now, I've come to value good rest, but even on the nights when I rested well, I'd rise the next morning, tired.

Things finally came to a head when I found myself taking a power nap before getting out into the morning commute. That's when I knew something was seriously wrong. I mean, think about it – you wake up, get dressed and take a nap ... before going to work ... not a good sign. So, I called my doctor and described what was going on, hoping to put this to rest once and for all. My timing couldn't have been better as I was due for a physical and unlike years past, I was looking forward to it.

I arrived and she took me through the usual battery of tests and to my surprise (and hers too), I have high blood pressure. The mood in the room screamed, "how could this be happening?" I mean, I work out regularly, run sometimes twice a day; eat well, drink plenty of water, rest, but I have high blood pressure. Something was amiss she said as she keyed my prescription into her laptop, and she promised me we would get to the bottom of it.

Later that week, my blood work came back, and she scheduled another appointment to review her findings. Turns out my thyroid wasn't functioning properly which caused a chain of events in my other organs. Since my thyroid wasn't operating at full capacity, the other organs weren't either. This in turn was causing my heart to work harder than it should have – hence the high blood pressure.

Problem solved, crisis avoided, new prescription ordered and ready for pickup. We sat there in her office, making small talk, waiting for my final paperwork to print off. I chuckled and told her about all the running I've done over the years including a marathon. She looked back at me with raised eyebrows and said, "there's no telling how much farther you'll be able to go now that you've got your insides fixed."

Look back over your life at all the places you didn't go and things you didn't do. Those misses didn't just happen, they started on the inside … the outside was just the manifestation. Here's the good news, you don't need to go to a doctor to fix those things – you can make that diagnosis and write that prescription yourself.

Starting today, write a prescription of victory in places wherever you used to feel defeat. During those challenging times we all encounter at some point or another, think can, instead of can't, replace might with will and watch how much more empowered you begin to feel. Whatever you want on the outside, starts on the inside and there's no telling how much farther you can go …

Once you get your insides fixed.

The Assembly Line

I financed my entire college education, every last bit of it working on an assembly line. That's right; no student loans, no financial aid, no grants – none of that. Just blood, sweat, tears … and a lot of heavy lifting. It was a tough, physically demanding job with lots of long hours, but looking back I wouldn't trade it for the world. On the line, as we called it, I was part of the final production team assembling commercial office furniture along with three others. There were two assemblers, one base builder and one final assemble and inspection person. Over the years the final production team changed a great deal with different people coming and going…but I was a mainstay. Then one day I looked up I was the only one left, manning that entire operation by myself as the others had left for other positions on the line.

Even though I was the only one working the area, the workload kept coming down the line at a rapid pace I might add. That's right the volume remained the same and so too did the level of production. There were days when I'd get a little angry and wonder to myself, "why isn't my manager sending someone to help." I later learned my manager never sent anyone to help because he knew I could handle it. A few years later I left that job as the time had come to put that degree to use. Yes, I finally landed the coveted corporate job we all dream of while toiling away in the college classroom, burning the midnight oil, and all that other good stuff. Upon arriving our workloads were broken down by industry with most employees receiving two or three at the most…but somehow or another, I ended up with eight.

Funny thing was that at the end of each week when we were called in for reviews…I was always 100% on-time with every assignment being submitted in a complete and orderly fashion. Most of my co-workers weren't so lucky as even though their workloads paled in comparison to mine, for some reason they were never quite able to match my productivity.

One day a manager from a manager from another team asked how I was able to manage my workload so well. Right then, a light bulb went off and it all began to make sense. All those years of working alone in that final production area at my former job … had prepared me to excel in my present job. I like to think, God saw what I had "coming down the line" and He purposely moved those other persons out of the way…to focus on preparing me for that something better that was to come…

If not today at some point in the future, you'll question why you're in a situation that on the surface looks too big for you to manage alone. Rest assured you're never alone and you're there because God knows you can handle it...Embrace it because it is a clear sign of God's love. He loves you so much that He's moved those other persons out of your way...because He wants you to be prepared for that something better that's "coming down the line ..."

Andy and Red

The Shawshank Redemption is one of my favorite movies. It's filled with powerful scenes, but the most powerful happens toward the end of the movie. Upon being released from the hole, the central character Andy Dufresne meets up with his best friend Red in the prison courtyard. Andy daydreams about what he would do if he were to ever be set free. He talks about the places he would go, the things he would do and the person he would become. Red in a moment of self-reflection daydreams a different daydream. On the inside, Red is what you might call "the man" able to broker deals and curry favor with guards and prisoners alike. He's the go-to guy at Shawshank but on the outside...his life prospects are dim and so too were his daydreams.

Before leaving one another's presence, Andy gives Red strict instructions on what he is to do should he ever get out. That night Andy escapes and some years later, Red is set free. While working a dead-end job and contemplating suicide among other things, Red finally decides to follow the instructions Andy gave him. He followed them down to the smallest detail and found a cryptic note that told Red where he could find Andy. The note said a lot of other things, but one-line hits me every time I see the movie. Andy wrote, "*I could use a man like you who knows how to get things*..." This wasn't just a line. Up until that moment Red was walking around a free man, still living in prison. But when he finally felt valued, although it took someone else to make him feel it...that's when he truly became free.

You'd be surprised at how many people are walking around free but in prison. Some of these people are in our midst every day. Still living behind walls that have been erected in some form or fashion but however, they manifest they keep them bound.

Sometimes all they need to hear is that someone special like you, believes in someone special like them; why don't you put that on top of your to-do list today. Because when they hear it, when they get that extra bit of encouragement, that something that says you are valued...

That's when they truly become free.

Pacesetting

I got my Halloween off to a rousing start in 2018. No tricks, no treats, ghosts, or goblins for me—instead, I ran in a 10K! A 10K is only 6.2 miles—I say only because in 2017, I ran in and completed a full-marathon—26.2 miles.

Although I completed that marathon, it came with a price. I found out one of my feet is slightly larger than the other. That might not be a problem walking around doing normal day-to-day activities—but when you're running that far, eventually, it becomes a problem.

Eventually it becomes a problem and it did and for that reason, I was forced to step away for a little while—but that Halloween weekend, I returned and oh how I looked forward to it. The people, the organizers, the family members cheering their family and you on…the energy; yeah, I missed that part of my life.

After what seemed like an eternity, we got the call to line up and run. Boom, the gun went off and so did we! In the beginning, there's always a huge cluster of runners seemingly stuck together, moving as one. As the race matures, that cluster of runners becomes a series of smaller groups or individuals as we all settle into our race.

I settled into mine and began cruising along. 1 mile down, 2 miles down, 3 miles down—hey I still got it. 4 miles…I'm getting tired, down, 5 miles—maybe I should walk the rest of the way, down. Somewhere during that 5th mile, I blocked out all the voices in my head telling me to stop and walk, gutted it out and finished.

I crossed the finish line, grabbed my medal and a bottle of water, high-fived everyone in sight and headed to my car.

As I was walking, a man's voice started to shout, "Sir…. sir…. sir" …

No way he's talking to me, so I just kept moving…but the voice came nearer and nearer until finally, there was a tap on my shoulder. I turned and there in front of me stood a person who up until that point, I'd never seen.

He extended his hand and said, "Thank you." I was confused but before I could ask what he was thanking me for, he told me all race long, he purposely ran behind me. He said he knew I was going to finish and if he could just stay close to me, he would too.

We laughed for a few minutes before congratulating each other one last time and heading out. As he backed up, he smiled broadly, pointed, and said, ***"You were my pacesetter man!"***

I had no idea.

You're running a race each day you walk out of your door. Each time you step foot into your office, their office, the mall, the store or wherever your daily takes you. But while you think you're just doing you—someone is watching. Yes, they're watching, on purpose, thinking that if they can just run behind you—they'll finish. Finishing might be becoming a better parent, a better friend, co-worker, or any number of things.

They're thinking if I can just stay close because they know you're going places...in life, making the right choices, doing the right things, placing others before you, living with honor and integrity – right things.

This week, when you think about quitting, when things get hard or those voices in your head tell you to stop, keep running...you may not know it...

But you're somebody's pacesetter.

Ali and Liston

In 2019, Louisville International Airport officially changed its name to the Louisville Muhammad Ali Airport. Ali is Louisville's favorite son, so changing the airports name to honor him was beyond fitting – even though he was afraid of flying.

Yes, the greatest fighter in history was afraid of riding on a plane. About the only thing he feared more than flying – was Sonny Liston. Oh, he talked a great game leading up to the fights that would define the early part of his career. Years later he admitted that it was just that as day after day he woke up terrified at the prospects of facing Liston.

Sensing his fear, but knowing it was too late to turn back, Angelo Dundee, Ali's manager, began planting seeds. From time to time, he'd remind Ali how much taller he was – Liston was just a shade over 6 feet while Ali stood nearly 6'4. Age was also on Ali's side as he was a full 12 years younger than his opponent – a fact his manager kept in the forefront of his guy's mind. When it came to footwork, Ali was a ring ballerina who floated like a butterfly. Liston on the other hand was a plodding, heavy-footed brawler earning him the nickname of – The Bear.

Fight night finally arrived and the bigger, stronger, younger, faster, Ali was having his way. Round 1, he peppered Liston with jabs, combinations, uppercuts, and hooks. Round 2 arrived and although Liston put up a better defense, Ali easily outpointed him. Round 3 was a mirror of the first two with the upstart contender handling the heavily favored veteran with relative ease.

At the end of Round 3, as Ali made his way back to his corner, a scary thing happened … he lost his vision, literally. As legend has it, Liston's corner spread some type of mysterious ointment on his gloves at the beginning of Round 3. Whatever it was eventually made its way into the eyes of Ali, robbing him of his sight.

Frustrated and frightened, Ali sat in his corner and told his manager to stop the fight because he couldn't see. Dundee was having none of it and instead of stopping the fight, he grabbed Ali and said, "I just need you to hold on until your vision returns"!

Round 4 saw Liston punishing the sightless Ali, pummeling him with body shot after body shot, wearing him down. "Hold on" said Dundee. With a minute left, Ali, who up until that point could see nothing, noticed a silhouette coming at him and began punching back. His corner drenched his face with water in between rounds 4 and 5 and he began to see clearly, re-establishing himself as the aggressor.

Round 6 arrived and there he stood, nearly 6'4 throwing lefts and rights from every conceivable angle, another one in the books. The bell rang for round 7 and Ali came charging out to meet his foe. Liston sat in his corner, looked up and spat out his mouthpiece. He knew he couldn't win because unlike others he had fought before who quit when their sight got blurry … Ali held on, until his vision returned.

There was a time in life when we were winning every round … and it wasn't even close. We threw jabs, uppercuts, hooks – punches were coming from every conceivable angle, and they were all landing. Money was right, career path was ahead of schedule, friends were there when we needed them and that special someone was more special than we could've ever imagined. Then round 3 ended and round 4 came. Life put something on its gloves… and things got blurry…

You might find yourself in a round 4 situation right now. If you do, you've got two choices. Cut off the gloves, throw in the towel and quit … or be like the greatest fighter who ever lived, come out and fight. If you come out and fight, something incredible will happen. You'll notice that with each passing round, things will get better. Yes, things will become clearer. Before you know it, you'll be standing taller, bigger, stronger, and faster than whatever it was that came to stop you. It might not seem that way in the beginning, but trust me, you win in the end…You've just got to hold on …

Until your vision returns …

Rain

The Atacama Desert located in Chile is one of the most mysterious places on the entire planet. Unlike most deserts the Atacama Desert is a very cold place with temperatures that dip into the single digits during the night; sometimes lower. Even during the day temperatures in this region barely creep above the freezing mark with wind chill factors that add to the bitter cold that this desert has come to be identified with.

What makes this place even more mysterious is the stillness... A stillness that is driven by the lack of life as the land is barren for hundreds of miles in all directions. There's no plant life, there's no wildlife, no insect life and there's no human habitation whatsoever in the Atacama Desert.

It's not the cold that keeps life from coming to the Atacama Desert as a man can build a home and generate enough heat to make it sustainable. Animals would follow once man has built an infrastructure and in theory so too would insects and plants, even if only in a limited fashion. No, the cold is not the problem in the Atacama Desert...the lack of water is. The Atacama Desert has gone decades without seeing a shower or a storm of any type. And since no showers ever come even for a little while, since no storms ever settle over the area for extended periods of time, since no rain ever falls in the Atacama Desert...nothing ever grows.

There was this one shower in my life that lasted for, oh just a little while. I got wet and complained but got through it. Not too long after that shower had ended there came this incredible storm, a monster of a storm. I found myself thinking I would give anything to go back to that shower...and that's when I realized how much I had grown. There was a time when that shower would have had me worried...now here I was thinking how easy it would be to overcome. I turned my attention back to the storm at hand and smiled knowing because of it and all of the rain it brought to my life...I'd grow. Learn to embrace the showers and storms, those dark, rainy periods of your life no matter how long they last. Because friend, without the rain falling in our lives...

Nothing would ever grow...

Bourgeoisie

When I was a child, history was one of my favorite subjects. Every single time the teacher would tell us to pull out our history books my face would light up. It didn't matter what period we were studying. It could be the Revolutionary or Civil War, the Alamo, or any parts in between—I loved history...almost as much as I loved Spelling.

Yes, I lit up during history, but I came to life whenever the time for Spelling was announced. I loved Spelling and let me tell you, I was good at it. I was so good that I taught myself how to spell all 50 states—backwards! When Spelling tests were given, I knew I would be the first to finish and my grade would always...always be 100. I loved Spelling. I loved it so much and I was so good that my 8th grade English teach entered me into the Spelling Contest. I remember practicing for hours upon hours and when the day of the contest came around, I just knew I would be the last one standing.

The contest started and we went through the early rounds. One by one, I watched as classmate after classmate fell by the wayside...leading to their exit. Me on the other hand, I was breezing through that thing. Every word the panel threw at me, I threw it back at them—spelled correctly!

The morning began with a packed room, but by the end of the hour, there were only 4 contestants left. In my mind, (and the minds of most) I was the favorite. My name was called, and I boldly stepped toward the panelist, thinking whatever word she had was no match for me. I steadied myself and announced I was ready...then she said it.

"Your word is BOURGEOISIE...spell it please" ...

I sounded it out, but it didn't register. I looked at the panelist and asked that it be used in a sentence: she complied—still, the word didn't register. The clock was ticking—here goes nothing...I spelled it loudly boldly thinking that maybe just maybe if I spoke in my strongest voice the spelling would come out right. When the last letter rolled out my mouth, the panelist looked at me and said, "Incorrect." The room was already silent, but it seemed to become more silent. My heart slowly sank before grabbing my things and walking out.

Later that day, I saw that panelist, who happened to be an English teacher at my school. We spoke for a few moments and before departing she looked at me and said, "I wish I could've taken that word back" ...

Words have power and unlike that spelling contest instance I referenced above...there is no incorrect. Say things like "I will", "I can", "I'll be fine", and watch how your life follows those words. The same is true on the other side of the coin. Speak things like "I won't" "It never will happen", "I'll never get over this", and your life will follow those words.

Be careful with the words you choose to speak into your life. Because once they're spoken...

You can't take them back...

The Mechanic down the Street

My neighborhood was an incredible place to grow up with a mix of people that made life interesting to say the least. Most of the families have moved on for various reasons but when we were all there together—it was truly special. There's a church directly across the street, a corner store with a dry cleaner, a gas station and, I promise you, an Oriental place that made hands down the best hamburgers...ever!

When it came to people it was just as special. My mother's three best friends all lived within shouting distance of one another—and back then, they'd have entire conversations without leaving their front porches. I can still remember them bellowing out responses up and down the street. It was a sight to see—and hear.

My buddies, pals, or "aces" as my father used to call them were right there too. Let me tell you, we became so close, so connected that we intuitively knew when to come out to get the fun started.

The neighborhood also had a mechanic a few doors down...but get this, his car sounded like at any point in time...it was going to fall apart. I mean, every single time he started it you'd hear backfires, loud groans and sounds only a car in distress could make. Funny thing I learned years later was that one of the guys used the sound of that car...as his alarm. Yes, when he heard that car starting, he knew it was time to get up for school. One morning I remember sitting down at the table, eating breakfast with my father and that car cranked up. That car cranked up and made all the noises it usually makes—and a few more. Without looking up my father said, ***"That guy is one heck of a mechanic."***

Confused, I looked at him and asked, "If he's such a good mechanic, why does his car sound like that?" No sooner than I could finish my question did my father put his fork down, take a nice sip of his coffee and say, "Because he's always so busy fixing someone else's car...he doesn't have time to fix his own." That's why his car looks that way, that's why it sounds that way. He keeps it in good enough shape to get by, but he never can get to it, because he's always on someone else's."

This week take a minute to check on that...mechanic in your life. I'm not talking about the one who fixes your car, I'm talking about the one whose always there to fix your, and chances are, a host of other lives...

You know the one that's always there when someone needs a shoulder to cry on, always has a little extra cash, never turns down a call and always returns a text, keeps a place for a friend to lay their head, is quick to fix a meal, will ride or die...or just listen.

That mechanic might even be you...

Check on them. Chances are, they might need a little work too. They're just so busy fixing everyone else's...that they can never find time to fix their own...

Let it Breathe

I never thought I would say this…but I really enjoy cooking. I mean, there was a time when I'd go all day with nothing more than a bag of chips and a soda—if that. But with this newfound love for cooking, the kitchen has become ***my domain – my sanctuary***. Cooking can be a lot of fun but as I said, I'm new to this. Yeah, I'm new to this and one day, I paid for it—dearly I might add. Baked salmon was on the menu that night along with a salad and what has become one of my go to options, a sweet potato.

The timer went off, alerting me that the fish was done. I moved toward the oven…and this is where the problem began. I reached in with one hand---with my phone up to my ear---and my eyes on the television…and POW! That's right, I burned the top of my hand. I had a potholder covering the inside, but the outside was exposed and bumped into the heating element at the top of the oven.

My hand immediately began to blister and swell and there wasn't a band-aid in the house. Now, here's where it gets interesting. I woke up early the next morning to drive to Killeen to take my father in for surgery. I hopped in the shower and, me being me, raked the soapy washcloth over my burned hand, ripping the blistering skin off. What was once a puffy brown irritation…had now become a rather gruesome sight.

I arrived in Killeen, picked my old man up and we headed to the hospital. The nurse and doctors came in and did their briefings and then left us alone. I sat down by the bed and my father noticed my hand. We laughed and talked about me becoming a cook and needing to pay more attention while doing it. I told him I didn't have any band-aid's, so I was just going to "borrow" a few from the hospital. He tilted his head ever so slightly and said, "I tell you what you do Lynn…let it breathe …"

Confused I looked back at him and asked, "What do you mean?"

"Don't go putting nothing over top of it—just leave it exposed to the air…let it breathe -- it'll heal faster that way." He was right. Although I finally bought some band-aids and wraps to cover it, because the thought of having an injury like that exposed worried me, each time I tried to use them…something felt off. So, I stopped trying and just let it breathe…and it healed.

🌲 🌲 🌲

This week, instead of covering up the hurt, the pain, the gruesome injury that life has thrown your way…let it breathe. Letting it breathe doesn't mean you have to tell everyone; you might not want to tell anyone. Letting it breathe might mean unwrapping the hurt, the pain, the injury and facing it by yourself. Expose it to the fresh air that comes from knowing that you matter, you have feelings…but those things are just parts of the journey.

The quicker you do, the sooner you'll be whole again. It'll leave a scar, but that scar will be a reminder of how far you've come, acknowledgement of a battle won. Starting today, professional, personal, wherever the hurt, the pain, the injury can be found, let it breathe…

It'll heal faster that way…

Body Blows

Julio Cesar Chavez and Meldrick Taylor...these two boxing legends fought arguably the greatest fight of the 1990's. At the time, Chavez was considered by most to be the best pound for pound fighter in the world. His record was unblemished with most of his victories coming by way of technical knockout, knockout or opponent submission. Taylor was the up and coming Olympic champion with a stellar amateur career and an amazing set of boxing gifts. He was polished and tough; Philadelphia born, bred, and trained in the mold of the great Joe Frazier who knew only one direction in the boxing ring: forward. When these two men met in March of 1990 it was billed as the Fight of the Century. From the first bell it was all action with each man giving as good as he took. The fight was fierce and lived up to its billing with the final round standing as one of the most controversial in boxing history.

With Taylor ahead on points Chavez connected with a series of blows that caused the fight to be halted with only 2 seconds left in the match. Referee Richard Steele was roundly criticized for his actions as he seemingly robbed Taylor of his chance to reign supreme on the world stage. When asked why he made this decision, Steele has always maintained the same position. He said that while the fans saw the seemingly minimal damage the blows Chavez was delivering to Taylor were causing on the outside, he on the other hand saw the incredible damage those blows were doing ...on the inside and in the ring, it's what's inside that counts.

The inside, body blows brought several of Taylor's internal organs significant, irreparable damage. The outside blows...they were damaging too but it's the inside that typically governs the outside; it's true in boxing, it's true in life.

All too often we go through life looking for approval, affirmation, and validation from someone else but in reality, that power is ours and ours alone; remember that. You really can change your life with your thoughts, so think positive, affirming thoughts each day; commit to doing that. Outside opinions come and go but remember, when they have come and gone, when it's all said and done ... it's what's inside that counts ...

If this Fence Could Talk

Although he still owns it my father no longer resides at the home my siblings and I grew up in. Yes, the Pearcey's have left Longview Drive but we've all agreed no matter where we go, Longview Drive will forever be in our hearts. No one lives there but whenever I'm in town, I'll still drop by the old house to reminisce, smile, and remember. From room to room I move thinking about all the good times we had while growing up in that small frame box.

My favorite place to go while living there was the backyard unless of course, it was time for me to cut the grass. Pushing that lawnmower down that hilly backyard and dragging it up; man, the thought of it all makes me sweat but you know, I wouldn't change it for the world. Yes, that backyard holds a lot of special memories. The big backyard on Longview Drive is home to a large concrete slab that my father poured and wrote the names of all of his children on. The backyard has a shed, a clothesline, trees that refuse to die and my favorite thing of all...the fence.

Yeah, that old fence holds a lot of stories. If you asked it to, it could tell you about all of those times my friends and I hopped over it to race down to the store for a comic book, a soda, a bag of chips, or ice cream. That fence could tell you about all of those nights it doubled as a shortcut after watching a high school football or basketball game. I promise you, that old fence man, that old fence could tell you everything you ever needed to know about a special time and a special place.

It could also tell you a story about a woman loving her man.

I remember it as clear as yesterday, what happened and how it happened. It was a sunny afternoon, I was only 5 and there stood my mother and I in the kitchen, her cleaning the house, me making a mess. Out of nowhere, a group of construction workers gathered on the other side of our fence. "Hmmm," was the sound she made before striding out to the yard to address the situation. I followed.

As it turns out the men were there to build a fence on the other side of ours but in order to do so, they would first have to attach a clamp to ours. Simple enough right? right...but before going forward, my mother kindly told them that they would have to get her husband's approval and he was not home. "We understand", they said. A little time passed and the worker who by this time I gathered was in charge came to our back door and politely asked if there was any word from my father. I remember my mother smiling and saying, "Not yet sir."

Morning turned to afternoon and each time he asked, he was met with the same reply. Finally, he and his team stood, arms crossed outside of our back door in a show of force, informing my mother that if it was ok with her, they were about to go ahead and complete their work. Now, these were big men, who looked nothing like us at a time when looking nothing like us was considered to be all the approval they needed.

This move might have worked on some, but it didn't stand a chance against my mom. I remember her slowly steadying her little frame, crossing her arms, and smiling a powerful smile before softly yet sternly saying…*" **I'm waiting…on my man …** "* That's when they got it. They didn't come back to that back door no more; no, they got it. She was only five feet tall; much smaller than the man in charge but from that point on oh there was no doubt whatsoever about who was in control.

A short time later my father pulled up in that brand spanking new Mercedes – the one she bought him…with cash, I might add at which time she informed him of the day's events. He went out, gave his approval and the men finished the job they had started earlier that morning. When he turned around, he was beaming. I didn't know how to describe the look on his face as he strode up the backyard to the door so back then I just called it happy…today I know it as love.

Yeah, it was love. It was love because he had a woman who had his back…it was love; it had to be; because his woman respected his place and made sure others did the same…Love because even today over forty years after her passing the mere mention of her name makes him melt…it's such a beautiful thing….love because no matter what she was facing she knew she had man who knew he was on his way…

That's why she waited on him….

You want that man to melt…you want that man to glow…Do you want that man to believe he can when the world says he can't…to find himself when he appears to be lost… Be there when he arrives. That's right, wait on him and remember the look on his face …

It's such a beautiful thing…

Dive!

As a child playing football with my friends was one of my favorite things to do. No matter if it was in-season or offseason, the playground across the street from my home always had something football-related going on. One day we might be out there playing kill the man with the ball. Another day we would be out running routes while claiming to be our favorite receiver. Then there were those days when we actually picked teams, lined up and played a game. And let me tell you those games were not just games...they were wars.

One Saturday afternoon sticks out in my mind as both sides were giving as good as they got. There were a lot of hard hits, a lot of trash talking and a ton of big plays...and I was involved in one. The older boys in the neighborhood acted as our coaches and after each play they huddled us up to design and run another. After one play that went absolutely nowhere, we huddled, and "Coach" went around and gave us each our assignment. He told me to split wide to the right, run a streak as fast as I could, and the ball would be there.

The ball was hiked, and I set out running my fastest. I looked over my left shoulder and here came that ball just like "Coach" said. But the more I looked back the more I began to realize I might not be fast enough to catch it. I was pumping my little 11-year-old arms and digging in with my little 11-year-old legs the best I could, giving serious chase but I was worried. "Coach" was too; so, he screamed the one word that made all the difference.

"Dive"!

I heard it, did it, caught it and scored. Touchdown!

Everybody is chasing something and no matter what it is rest assured it's within your reach. But sometimes we miss out on catching it because we fail to realize that in order to do so; we're going to have to give a little more. We give chase, running as fast as we can pumping our arms and grinding our legs but when it becomes obvious that we aren't fast enough, we quit.

Oh, but if we had just been willing to dive. If we had just been willing to dive...If we had just been willing to dive, we would've gotten that job. If we had just been willing to dive, we would still be in business. If we had just been willing to dive, she or he and we would've stayed put. Oh, if we had just been willing to dive...The next time you feel yourself chasing something that seems to be getting away from you; chasing something you know was meant for you, remember why you began running in the first place. Keep chasing it and when it seems as though you have truly given it all you have to give, instead of quitting... Dive!

It'll make all the difference...

Be Still

Awhile back, I spent an afternoon hanging out with my father as he continues to recover from a recent health scare. His doctors are amazed that after all of the poking, prodding, cutting, removing, on and on, he has yet to take any of his pain medication. I guess that's that old soldier in him rising up to do battle, refusing to be defeated. When will the battle learn that the old soldier can't be beaten? I got there just a little after 11 and as soon as I sat down, we began laughing and talking like two old friends who just happened to be father and son. No television, no radio, no phones ringing; none of that, just words. If you can name it, we probably touched on it. From football to politics, the job market, the housing market, the weather and then out of the blue he asked…

"Man, you remember that day we was out there running and that great big ole dog came at us?"

My father runs alone nowadays but there was a time when he and I were running buddies. We mostly ran together on the weekends during the school year. At the crack of dawn, he'd poke his head in my room to see if I were awake then softly ask me if I wanted to hit the road with him. I would always say yes, hop out of bed, clean myself up, throw on some shorts or sweats and we would head out together.

One particular morning run I'll never forget. We were chatting it up, and running down Highway 190 in Killeen, Texas; a route dotted with car lots, fast food joints and body shops…when out of nowhere we heard a vicious growl. We stopped our chatter, stopped in our tracks, and turned around and that's when we saw it, a huge German shepherd.

By the time we spotted him, the dog was no longer just growling; it had now begun barking and charging directly toward us. My instincts kicked in and I turned to run but as soon as I did, he grabbed my shirt and said, ***"Be still."*** Be still I thought. We have a German shepherd bearing down on us and he's telling me to be still. I wasn't sure what he saw, but all I saw was danger.

As the dog got closer, my father made a bold move; the kind of move only a father would make. He calmly stepped in front of me, bent down and reached out his hand towards the oncoming dog. The dog kept coming and got closer and closer until it finally stopped…and started licking his outstretched hand.

I look back on that day and realize that even though by this time I was well on my way to being bigger and stronger than him, I was still his child and he was still my father. And because I was his child and he was my father he wasn't going to let any harm come to me.

After that experience, I was ready to turn back, but he started running again and beckoned for me to follow. When I caught up to him the first thing he said was, "Trust me; no matter how bad it might look, I'm gone' take care of you…"

You ever see danger heading your way? Vicious, barking, growling danger. Friend know that you have a Father in heaven already standing in front of you, very much ready, very much willing, and very much able to take on whatever or whoever is coming your way. So, the next time you see danger instead of breaking and running...be still. Be still and trust in your Father because no danger is too great for Him and no matter how bad the situation or circumstances might look...

He's gone' take of you...

The Shedding

I've settled back into my run routine here of late as I continue to transition into this new phase of life without my old man. He introduced me to the road, but with so much going on with his health these past few months, I got away from it. With him now residing in a better place, I'm back out there just as he would've wanted. We always had this idea that one day, we'd run a race together. That dream never came true, but after each race, the first call I'd make was to him. I'd tell him how this tip or that tip paid off, at just the right time and in just the right place. A country boy, he loved hearing about the tall buildings and beautiful neighborhoods the race road took us through. He loved all those things, but what he found to be most fascinating was the part of the race, was The Shedding.

I only run long races during the fall and winter seasons, at his direction of course. I remember him telling me many times, "don't fool around and run out there in that heat; you'll burn up." So, with that, my long races always take place during the colder months. Just like the majority of the runners, when I line up, I'm layered up. Hat, gloves, sweatshirt, hoodie, and anything else I can find to keep me warm are with me when that starters gun sounds.

But as the race unfolds and our bodies begin to warm, The Shedding ... begins. The first trickle of sweat runs down the runner's cheek, it's telling them the warm hat is no longer needed ... so they gently drop it on the street. The hoodie that once fought off the cold north wind, is slowly unzipped and left on the sidewalk. A few miles later, the same fate befalls the sweatshirt that hid underneath that hoodie. Sweaty palms mean gloves must come off and those too are dropped without a second thought. With shedding in full swing, the most beautiful part of the race begins. People lining the streets rush to gather those things left behind. In the days to come, shelters and charities are inundated with hats, gloves, jackets, and warm clothing – things that were dropped during the race, that are eventually passed on to those who need them for theirs.

I once worked at a funeral home and as a result, I became the point person for my father's service. We arrived early and I immediately sought out and began coordinating with the Director, making sure everything went off without a flaw. When it became apparent things were on course, she left me alone and that's when visitors began stopping by.

A local track coach came in, noticed the resemblance, smiled, and said, "you're Mr. Pearcey's son, aren't you?" "Guilty" was my response. We laughed shook hands and then he told me a story. He said one day he was prepping his running club for a workout and across the way, he saw my father running. Coach beckoned for him to come over and when he arrived, the coach asked if he'd mind sharing a few words with the kids. The coach didn't remember all that was said, but what he did remember was that after hearing from my father, they had the most incredible workout ever. That said it all ...

A neighbor stole away from work just long enough to view his body and sign the guest book for herself and her son. She came over and we had the best talk as she shared stories about what my father meant to her and the lessons that she learned just from being in his presence. "Whenever I was down and felt like I couldn't make it – I thought about your daddy and how even at his age he was still out there running!" She said it kept her going ...

It only takes six to carry a casket, but we had a pool of pallbearers, ready, willing, and honored. I remember calling one, the one who my father would've insisted be there ... and hearing him say he couldn't. I remember pain in his voice as he told me he had family obligations of his own that conflicted with ours. By the end of that brief call I could tell his heart was filled with sorrow. A few hours later, he called back saying there had been a mistake and he could in fact serve! I will never forget the excitement, joy, and love in his voice as he told me how much my father and our family meant to him and promised no matter what, he'd be there. By the end of that brief call and just be hearing the sincerity in his voice ... my heart became filled with joy ...

In the days to come I'll continue picking up things my father left along the way, things he shed during his race. What warms my heart the most is to know that others will too. As you navigate the streets of life, running your race, don't forget to do the same. Because the things you shed, the things you no longer need for yours ... could be just the thing someone else needs for theirs ...

Boy

Moving to a new neighborhood means finding new running routes. No worries, that's actually one of the best parts of the move. Most days, I have no idea which direction I'm going, I just take off. One day I might go left, the next right, the day after I'll twist and turn until it feels right. While I never know how I'll start, I always know how I'll end. More importantly, I know who'll be waiting for me,

His name is Boy.

Boy is the dog five houses down and let me tell you, he's the coolest dudes ever. Only a pup at the time, he was the first to greet me when I moved in. Even though he's grown up to be a pretty big boy, he still shows the innocent ***"puppiness"*** that was on display during our first meeting.

At the end of each of my runs, I make it a point to stop by his fence and spend a few minutes with Boy. He'll see me coming from a distance and start running back and forth, jumping up and down, with an excited bark. No matter how far I've run or how tired I might be, I'll make my way over and spend a few minutes, rubbing his head or stomach; whichever he prefers. If there's a toy within reach, I'll grab it and toss it around a time or two before rubbing him on the head and going my way.

A small pond sits in back of the row of houses on my street, separating us from those on the other side. There's a walkway that wraps around it that ends right by my backyard. Monday, I got distracted by a phone call and took that route instead of the normal one that passed me right by Boy's house.

All while I was on that call, I heard this barking in the background. The further I walked in the opposite direction, the more barking I heard. I finally looked to my left to see where all this barking was coming from … and there was Boy, on the other side of the pond, running around in his backyard, jumping up and down, trying his best to get my attention. Without hesitation, I made my way over to his house where we spent a few minutes catching up. The tone of his bark and wag of his tail as I headed off told me that just by showing up, I made his day.

Truth be told, he made mine too …

If you listen closely, there's someone in your life, calling out to you. It could be a co-worker, a family member or close friend waiting patiently for you to show up. Make it a point to not become so distracted that you miss out on hearing them. An encouraging text or email, a quick chat on the

phone or a shared laugh -- the joy you bring through that small gesture could be just the thing they need to make their day.

Truth be told, it might make yours too ...

Final Score: 6-0

I love football and that should come as no surprise, especially if you know me, even in passing. It doesn't matter if it's a game between two college rivals on a brisk Saturday afternoon, a matchup of winless teams featuring undersized schoolboys on a warm Friday night, or a bunch of millionaires playing for a trophy on the last Sunday of the season...if they're playing, I'm watching.

Yes, I love the game but over the course of my illustrious football career I scored a grand total of...drum roll please...one touchdown. That's right, in all those years of grunting, grinding, and toiling under the hot Texas sun, I tasted the end zone only once...but I'll never forget that game. Yes, when you played at 5'3 130 pounds, (But a year later, you're 5'9, 195 pounds...go figure) you tend to hold onto those memories.

It was in Austin and Anderson High was the opponent. Now, even though it was only a junior varsity game, I must say there was a pretty nice crowd on hand for what turned out to be a stiff battle with both sides showing up with their best stuff! Back then wide receivers, the position that I played, were for the most part, nothing more than glorified, undersized blockers as the game almost totally revolved around running backs. That game did too but on this one play, this one incredible play...the game revolved around me.

Man, I can remember it like it was yesterday; as soon as that play arrived in the huddle, I knew I had a chance to do something big because I had been setting the defensive back up for that play, that very play all...game...long. Wing Right 80-Quick Out and Up was the call and the instant the ball was snapped, I set off...on a mission. I burst out of my stance, gave a hard inside jab, and went into an out route. The defensive back bit on that out...and up I went, full speed ahead, in a dead sprint, determined to get open and even more determined not to let anyone stop me.

I kept running and looking back and kept running and looking back and out of nowhere, ***there came a perfectly thrown, tight spiral***. Without breaking a stride, the ball fell perfectly into my hands and I galloped the remaining 20 yards into the end zone for what ended up being the game's only score! It was the best feeling in the world as I turned around to see teammates with raised arms racing toward me.

We won that game 6-0 and to the surprise of no one, Coach recognized me as the player of the game, but he also gave me a stern life lesson that I carry with me to this very day. He congratulated me on the touchdown but said instead of one, I should've had three. I couldn't see my face but I'm quite sure I had the most curious look as I wondered exactly which game, he was watching...and that's when he launched into me.

"That hitch pass that we threw out to you in the flat and the only thing standing between you and another touchdown was some kid who looked like he had no business on the field; you let him stop you."

He went deeper. "Pearcey, how about that post pattern? I've seen you catch up to balls like that all day; everyday, in practice but you weren't able to get to that one …" Coach got quiet and I stayed silent but before walking away he lightly tapped me on my shoulder and said, "You missed out on those other two scores because you became content son…don't ever let that happen to you again."

There's a certain danger, a limiting quality associated with the word content. We get a promotion at the work and become content…stop coming early stop staying late, allowing someone else to shine, losing sight of the fact that the promotion could have been the start of a career, not just a job.

We find the right one, him or her. The wedding comes and goes and the little things that made us fall in love go by the wayside. He no longer courts her; she no longer believes in him. What would've been a happily ever after becomes a place of tolerance, not love.

You make a baby, hey if you're blessed, you might make children. You might make children, but sometimes parents become so content making children … that they forget to honor that blessing by building strong young people. You can't go back and change the times it happened before, but moving forward, be leery of becoming content.

It's the only thing stopping from living life to the fullest.

Re-purposing

Years ago, I remember having what I can only describe as an eye-opening conversation with a client. He had a very interesting non-profit focused on green energy and environmental conservation based in the Midwest and came to me in need of a business plan. The business had a lot of different facets and he had a ton of ideas on how to protect the environment. They were simple, but when he explained them to me, I can honestly say I was blown away. Among all of the ideas that he rattled off, the one that most caught my attention was water re-purposing. Through this concept, water from storms is captured in barrels and re-purposed in a variety of areas including gardening, landscaping, lawn care, laundry, and other common household chores.

I was amazed and he could tell. I laughed and told him "I guess I've just become so used to turning on the faucet and getting what I need …" He laughed at me and said, "Most of us have but around here at the first sound of thunder, first sight of lightning we get our barrels out; we don't waste no storms!"

You know, a lot of times the waters that fall during the storms of life aren't meant to be used during the season that they fall in. What's even more interesting is that a lot of times the waters that fall during these storms aren't even meant to be used by us. That water that falls somehow, some way…somewhere is meant to be re-purposed… A storm might come in a relationship…but the waters that fall can be re-purposed and used on the job. A storm might come on the job…but the waters that fall can be used again, they can be re-purposed to raise a stronger child. A storm might come on the playing field…but can be re-purposed and used in everyday life. The next time you hear thunder…the next time you see lightning…the next time a storm comes your way; before you run for cover…get your barrels out… and for God's sake …

Don't you waste no storm!

Raining on the Outside

To say North Texas is exploding with growth would be an understatement. It seems on every corner, red light, and intersection there's something being built. It might be a subdivision, a strip mall, a school, or a hospital but you can always see someone on the outside building...except for on the days when it rains. On the days when it rains ***no work can be done outside*** because the water prevents it. In some cases, even days after the rain has ceased building on the outside is prohibited due to the amount of moisture in the air.

On the surface when we drive by those buildings and see no work being done outside, the reality of it all is that work is still being done; it's just being done on the inside. Yes, contractors are inside laying a solid foundation. You might not see them but they're on the inside hanging and running the wiring that will power the structure once it's been completed. Men and women, hard workers are hard at work on the inside painting walls, hanging pictures and beautifying. When you stop and think about it, it makes sense. It makes perfect sense because no matter how good a building might look on the outside, if it doesn't have what's necessary to drive it on the inside, it will have all been for nothing.

Rainy days, long stretches of rainy days often show up in life and in all too many cases we sit back and stop building. We let the water stop us because all we focus on is the outside. We focus on the body, the hair, the clothes, the nails...never once considering that it's raining on the outside because we are being called to do work...on the inside. On the inside is where you build the foundation that keeps you grounded in the tough times. The inside work, yes that's where the wiring is hung and run that powers you toward your destiny. Inside, not outside, is where you begin to hang pictures...envisioning yourself for where you want to be and how beautiful it will be when, not if, you reach there. The next time life seems to be sputtering, veering off track and being less than what you want it to be, don't waste your time focusing on the outside.

It's the inside that's calling you...

Mom and the hill

Every single time I take a visit to my hometown, I'm struck by all of the things that have changed but in my mind's eye, remain the same. My father doesn't live in the old neighborhood anymore – but that neighborhood still lives in me and nothing has changed.

There's the playground at the elementary school across the street where old friends would gather for games of 21, horse, and play pickup games. There are no rims, backboards, or swings there anymore as the school has now become an annex. But the memories we made and the bonds we built go beyond games, balls, or any piece of playground equipment. Those bonds will last forever.

Marlboro Heights Missionary Baptist Church sits directly in front of our old house. Each day that church played chimes telling the time to all who could hear. Each night at 9:30, those church chimes would play the most beautiful song; I never found out the name of that song, but I can still hum it just the same. On most nights, my crew would gather not too far from the church, talking, dreaming, playing catch, and just having the most innocent fun. They don't hold church there anymore as they built a new one a few miles away. But that church, that place, will forever be woven into the fabric of our hearts.

Those places and countless others hold a special meaning for me, but none can compare to the hill that leads to the old grocery store behind our house. It's not quite the hill it used to be but it's still there nonetheless and has a special meaning. When I was around 5, just about every day as my siblings and father were at school and work, my mother and I would walk down to get groceries then walk back up to bring them home. The walk down was no problem as she held my little hand, we talked, laughed, she told me things she needed and asked me not to forget (knowing full well that she wouldn't).

There was the trail of water that marked the midpoint of the parking lot that we used to jump over. Who could ever forget the lamp post? There's no way you could – the one with the square base painted bright yellow, announcing itself for all to see. If you looked to the right, there stood the alley ... big and bold, filled with workers, good people, stocking the store we were about to enter. Yes, I guess you could say our walks to the store were pure bliss.

The walk home was different. For a small woman like her and a small child like me, the walk home...could at times be tough. There was no plastic back then, just paper and I can vividly remember the days she struggled to carry those bags and wishing I were big and strong enough to help. So many days I've stared at that hill wishing we could have just one...more...walk. I would gladly carry it all ... every last bag.

I remember seeing her struggle but what I recall the most is that no matter how much those bags held, no matter how much they challenged her, or how out of breath her little body became...is that she always found enough strength to hold onto my hand.

Our neighborhood is nestled just off a highway and cars would zoom through the parking lot and streets with reckless abandon. Stray German Shepherds, big ones, roamed the roads and racism was so much more overt.

But as I sit and think about that hill, I can honestly say in all those days when those things and more were swirling around us, I was never once afraid. In fact, in all the days before and all of the many days that have passed since, I can honestly say that the palm of her hand...was the safest place I've ever been...

Mothers are the most beautiful people God ever created. If you're blessed enough to have yours, spend some time with her. Think about all of the hills the two of you have climbed together when no matter what load she was carrying; she always found the strength to hold onto your hand.   I'm sure you'll agree...

It's the safest place...you've ever been...

Daddy was a Kicker

I know just about everything there is to know about my father. In the 7th grade, for some reason I'm still not sure why, I memorized his social security number. Shirt, suit, waist ... I know those. Size 9 in running shoes, 9.5 in dress shoes – I know those feet.

His favorite food, soul food of course. Give him a pot of greens, a big bowl of beans, a pan of cornbread and something cool – not cold, to wash it down and he's in heaven. Yes, when it comes to that old man, chances are I know it – in some cases better than he does.

So, imagine my surprise a few years back as we sat doing what we do best, watching a football game when out of nowhere, he tilted his head, looked over his glasses and said, ***"did you know I was a kicker in college?"***

No ... I didn't ...

This time last year, I found myself standing in a hot parking lot taking a call from my father's doctor, hearing news no child wants to hear. The old man had cancer, problematic in and of itself, but age complicated his diagnosis. Chemo was used in times past, but the doctor confided in us that if he were treated with the recommended doses, it would do more harm than good. So, with chemo out, the path entailed rehab and transition. The rehab part we got – transition, was a little more complicated. Transition, as it was explained to me, meant preparing him and the family for his passing.

When the doctor gave him the update, per his usual, my father took it in stride. On the day we checked him into the rehab center, he couldn't walk. That's right, the guy who used to run from one end of the city to the next had to be wheeled into the facility. "I'll be alright", is what he told anyone within earshot.

Week after week he'd lay in that bed, unable to walk. With no measurable progress, the rehab center sent him home for what was to be the transition phase. He got home and for quite some time he was still confined to a bed. Day after day he continued to lay there, but he also continued to tell anyone who would listen that despite the doctor's prognosis ... he would be alright.

The rehab center sent a wheelchair home with him and one day, he eased into it and began wheeling himself around the house. We heard the news and thought ... he's getting alright. On Father's Day, we traveled home to see him and by this time he had become a pro with that wheelchair, twisting and turning this way and that way. Knowing him the way I do he's probably got a five-speed transmission or order for that thing.

A few weeks back I stopped in to spend the afternoon with him. I rang his doorbell and through the glass door, I could see him wheeling his way to me. He got almost all the way to the door – then he got up out of the wheelchair, walked those precious last few steps and let me in the house.

A great big smile flashed across his face as we embraced, not as firm as it used to be, but far stronger than it had been of late. Before letting go he patted me on the shoulder and said, "look at your boy ... I told you I'd be alright."

All those weeks that turned into months, his body was laying in that bed ... but his mind wasn't. In his mind, he saw himself walking which is why he can. "Before you come down here next time Lynn, pick me up a pair of those nice running shoes will you please, you know my size." He sees himself running, from one end of the city to the next, just like he used to. I believe he will.

Whatever it is you're going through right now, see yourself coming through it. See yourself and it, whatever it is, being "alright" ... and it will be so. About my father, he's doing better than alright ...

That boy ... is still kicking!

Some days, your Mother Needs you

As a child, I absolutely loved being outside, ripping and running with my friends. Honestly, I can still hear the sounds of kids laughing and screaming, bikes zooming down sidewalks, marbles, jacks, games of tag, so on and so forth. You seldom hear that anymore, but back in my day, that fun and more was everywhere.

I loved being outside, but I vividly recall my mother asking me to stay in with her a lot. There was no mention of why and I didn't protest, throw a fit or disobey – but it was hard. While all the other kids from the neighborhood were within earshot, having the time of their lives, I sat with my mother.

We talked about school and all the things I was learning. If we got hungry, we'd make peanut butter and jelly sandwiches – without the peanut butter, because at the time, I hated peanut butter. There were only a handful of channels back then and every now and again, we'd luck up and find a cartoon or two to share.

At some point, she'd squeeze me real tight, pat me on the behind, and kiss me on the forehead and release me to childhood. Off I went to the swings, the sandbox, riding a bike, throwing a ball -- doing the fun things kids used to do. I'll always remember waving goodbye to her as I ran out to join the playful fray – as if you really need to wave goodbye...when you're only 30 feet away.

Over the years, I've thought a lot about those days, those afternoons when everyone else was outside playing, but I was being kept inside. My mother knew something I didn't. She realized her time was short and wanted to soak up every drop of happiness this side had to offer.

I'm glad I didn't cry or protest, pout or show any sign of not wanting to be there. As I've gotten older, I figured it out, it took some time, but I figured it out. I came to understand why it meant so much to put off riding my bike so we could talk about school. I figured out why we sat and watched cartoons that even as a child I had absolutely no interest in...but I watched anyway.

Those bikes were going to be ridden, those balls were going to be thrown, someone was going to be tagged, and those swings were going to always have a passenger ... the outside would be just fine. But as I think back during long runs, walks, drives or just time spent alone, I realize the reason she kept me so close during those days was ... because she needed me more...than the outside did.

Check on your mother today ... check ... on ... your ... mother ... today. Text her, call her, go see her. Write her a letter, send her a card, take her out to dinner and claim that precious part of life. We spend so much time on the outside, stopping only to love on our mothers when we need her.

Today, put the outside on hold and understand that sometimes…your mother needs you …

Waiting on You

I never liked eating when I was a little kid, in fact I hated eating with a passion. Until I was oh, around 5, I thought breakfast, lunch, and dinner were curse words and I didn't hold the word snack in much higher regard. Even when my mother was alive, she'd have to coax me into eating my meals; despite the fact that she was an incredible cook.

Just like most kids there were some things like hot dogs, her homemade apple pies with the woven crusts, and ice cream sandwiches that needed no selling. But for the most part, I was an extremely light eater with my mother commenting about once per day that I "barely ate enough to keep a small bird alive." When she passed my father took over the household cooking duties and his menu, was far more limited than hers.

Gone were the homemade pizzas, biscuits, pies, and cakes. Gone were the fried chicken, pork chops, French fries, and casseroles. In their place a steady diet of greens, beans, okra, baked this, baked that, squash, and peas. Those were the foods he was raised on and knew how to prepare and as a result, those were the foods that comprised our menu in the years after my mother's passing.

Now, my father had several rules in his house but two in particular stood out. The first one was that you had to bathe each morning when you woke up and each night before bed. The second was you eat everything on your plate. The first one, I had no problem with…

It's the second one that gave me fits…

Over the course of my young life, he and I would have several mealtime tests of wills; him telling me I was not leaving the table until I cleaned my plate…me begging him to let me get down. One meal in particular where I absolutely refused to eat included lima beans, collard greens, sweet potatoes, baked chicken, and cornbread. Sounds delicious now but for a little kid who simply hated eating and a father who wouldn't let him down until he did…it was the perfect storm for a dinner table showdown.

So, we sat there and sat there and sat there, long after everyone else had got up and left; like two gunslingers in an old Western, him reading his newspaper…me eye-level with a plate full of food. After about a half an hour or so, he took the newspaper down, looked over at me and said…

"Waiting on you …"

At that point I figured I was going to lose…again; so, I got my fork and shoved a load of lima beans into my mouth. I chewed them up and went back in for another forkful. I finished chewing those and went back in for another forkful…and out of nowhere; another fork…started digging in my greens. I looked up and to my surprise…it was my father.

He finished off the greens and I finished off the lima beans. He pushed the smaller piece of chicken my way and took the bigger piece for himself. We split the sweet potatoes down the middle and I can still remember him cutting that piece of cornbread with his fork and giving me the curved side. We finished it up and he never said a word after we were done; he just shot me a dry smile and nod of the head.

All that time I spent sitting there thinking I was in it alone only to find out that my father was waiting on me to do my part so he could start doing his.

Hey, the next time you feel like you are facing a situation that you can't overcome, stop and remember ... God is ready to dig in and help bring you the victory; ready to do His part...

He's just waiting on you...

Inventory

For 10 years, I worked at a manufacturing plant, building commercial office furniture and I can honestly say it was one of the best times of my life. Five sometimes six days, ok, most of the time six days a week we'd work 10-hour schedules building a number of chairs and tables and doing everything in between. From lifting and packing to shipping and receiving; from upholstering and repairing to assembling and re-assembling, if you can name it, chances are we did it. It was a tough job but looking back, I can honestly say I grew so much as a person and learned a lot of valuable life lessons while at that job. One of the lessons that sticks with me the most took place, during inventory.

Each year the plant would shut down operations to take inventory with the results being reported back to accounting and finance to help determine the overall profitability of the company. The day inventory began our boss would assign each one of us an area to assess. Inventory was a long, tedious, and boring process that a lot of employees simply dreaded as we had to manually count each nut, bolt, staple, and piece of material in the entire building. I can't remember a single soul looking forward to taking inventory. So hated was this time of the year that some employees would show up for work and then go out of their way to do as little as possible. They'd hide, take long bathroom breaks, take long lunch breaks, fake family emergencies, and a host of other tactics, all geared toward getting out of work. So, one year, the boss called us all together and made a pretty profound observation. He said, "Guys some of you are putting more effort toward not working than you would be if you actually did the work; so why not just do the work?" Light bulbs went on all over the room...

You know some of us put more effort toward not believing something better is on the way than we do in believing that something better is on the way. The truth is if we would just use that wasted energy we expend not believing and channel it into something positive...channel it into a believing mindset, we'd soon find out that nothing is beyond our reach. Remember no matter what area of your life you're looking for a breakthrough in, it can happen...

But only if you choose...to believe...

The Irony of the Chains

From everything that I have read, seen, and studied and heard, slavery was nothing short of hell on Earth for the brave souls that were forced to endure it. It was the darkest period in human history and its residual effect still in many cases reverberate to this day.

The institution was filled with several ironies. For example, slaves were forced to cook full course meals for their masters...but were fed scraps unfit to be consumed by animals. Slaves built palatial mansions that still dot the southern landscape. But that same southern landscape is also dotted with primitive shacks – used to house slaves, built by slaves.

Slaves were brought over from Africa in chains. Slaves were locked up at night in chains. Slaves were tortured in chains. Slaves were forced to work while being restrained by chains. And the cruelest of all ironies is that these chains that were being used to capture, lock up, torture, and restrain were made...by the slaves themselves. Make no mistake about it there were other factors that kept them bound but the chains themselves were a powerful reminder of their status and one that haunted them daily.

Some of us are being held back daily by chains...and just like those slaves I referenced above...they're chains we ourselves have made. We use them to lock us up at night...and they deprive us of our dreams when we rise. We allow them to torture us throughout the course of the day...day after day. They restrain us at work and cause us to miss out on valuable career opportunities. They restrain us in our business and those businesses never grow to become what they should be. My hope for you is that you'll break whatever chains you've created that have left you bound. Be they at work, at home, in relationships or any other part of your life. Great man, Incredible woman, you have been bound long enough...***it is truly time to set yourself free...***

Thanksgiving and Credit Cards

I hardly use them anymore, but I remember getting my first credit card in the mail like it was yesterday even though it was way, way back in 1990. I was a student at the time and thought there was no way I'd ever get approved and even when that bright, shiny, green Mastercard showed up, I wondered if it were real. So, there it sat on my dresser for the better part of two months -- it looking at me and me looking at it until I finally got up the nerve to make my first purchase; a t-shirt from The Gap. Yes, that "T" was my first purchase but let me tell you, it was far from my best.

Most of us can attest to the fact that when a young person moves away from the comforts of home it can be a struggle in ways we could never have imagined. Bills, bosses, full-time jobs, and the rigors of young adult life are all a part of that all-important growth phase that some pass while others fail. In most cases, so too are second or third-hand automobiles and as fate would have it, I worked with a guy who owned one. To say that he had a piece of a truck would be an insult to the phrase "piece of a truck". The truck he drove was what my father calls a maybe.

Maybe it will start.
Maybe it will get you there.
Maybe you will get home.
Maybe the wheels will fall off, maybe they won't...maybe, maybe, maybe.

It was a maybe, but it was all he had, and he and his wife wanted desperately to make it home to San Antonio for Thanksgiving; a four-hour drive from Arlington, where we both lived at the time. But that piece of a truck wasn't nearly enough to get them there...and that's when I pulled out that credit card and made the best purchase ever.

He paid me back the following pay period just like he promised he would but years later, he paid me yet again. He said, "Man I really needed to see my mom that year and if you hadn't come through, I didn't know what I was going to do. Thanks for being there brother." It must've been three, maybe four years after the fact and I had no idea the impact it had on him, but it made it all the more gratifying to know that I was there when he needed me.

Here around town our paths have crossed every so often and let me tell you, he's come a long way. Each time we see each other, we laugh, he asks how things are and before we go, he'll say, "Brother are you good, you need me?" His asking me if I'm good or if I need him is genuine; it's sincere. I've never taken him up on his offer and probably never will, but it does my heart good to know that his heart still remembers. Still remembers the best purchase I ever made with that credit card...which happens to have become one of my best Thanksgiving memories.

Take a look around and I'm sure you can find someone in your midst less fortunate than you. Don't be afraid to extend yourself or share in whatever capacity you're able. You'll be amazed by the way it impacts their life.

But I promise you, you'll be even more amazed by the way it impacts yours...

Fight for the Shore

From the moment a slave party raided an African village, there was conflict. In most instances, no one in the village had ever seen a person who looked like the slaver so their appearance in and of itself was a shock. But once the shock wore off and they began to understand the gravity of the situation, their instincts kicked in—and they began to fight.

The two greatest weapons in the arsenal of the slaver were the element of surprise and gunpowder. African lore is filled with stories of them being fierce warriors and that they were—but even the strongest warrior is weakened when he's caught off guard. And no matter how skilled he, she, they may have been, their spears were no match for gunpowder.

When the smoke cleared, and the battle, the first battle that is, ended the next phase of horror began—the dreaded march to the slave castles. In some cases, this trip could take months and cover hundreds of miles. Upon arrival, the seasoning process continued. That's right, seasoning because ***no person is born a slave;*** they must be forced into that role and in these castles, that process began in earnest. Here, the person was slowly transformed into a thing.

After what must have felt like an eternity, filled with degradation, humiliation, and outright anger, the boarding of ships began—and this is where the second and final battle took place. The second was even more fierce than the first because the plight of both parties depended on the outcome. The slaver knew that if he could get far enough out into the ocean, his mission was all but accomplished. Their fight was rooted in dollars and cents because each slave delivered meant more of a profit was made.

The Africans, on the other hand, fought for an entirely different reason of course. Historians say the African "fought for the shore". They fought for the shore because they knew that if they allowed that ship to get too far away, to the point where they could no longer see their beautiful homeland...their end was near.

They fought for the shore because it represented the promises of life...
They fought for the shore because the shore held all their dreams...
They fought for the shore, with one eye on their enemy and the other on their beloved Africa...
They fought for the shore because they understood that if they lost sight of it...

All hope would be lost...

Some of us are being marched into castles and onto ships filled with despair, soon to be sent out into an ocean where every fire that ever burned inside of us will soon be dashed.

It doesn't have to be this way so this week instead of sitting by, watching the promises of life pass you by...fight for the shore. When the walls begin to close in and you find yourself becoming the thing someone else imagined instead of the person you always dreamed you'd be...fight for the shore...With one eye on your enemy and the other on your beloved dreams...fight for the shore and refuse to lose sight of all you imagined life to be.

Hope isn't lost, your dreams haven't passed you by, your time is still now but for all these things to come to pass you must be willing...

To fight for the shore...

The Pictures

Slowly but surely the house is being decorated. A chair here, a comforter there, new pillows, paint for this room, that one, and the next, desk, vase, books– yes, things are really beginning to come together. Even those areas that still remain empty have already been filled in my mind. Yes, from the time I walked in this house I knew exactly what I wanted to do with every space – with the exception of that great big wall in the entry. The wall is huge and over these last few months, no matter what I've placed there, nothing could stand up to it. From chairs to tables to ottomans and lamps ... they were no match for it. They were no match, but the wall deserved attention. Each time I passed it, I heard it saying in an almost audible voice, **"honor me."** "I'm doing my best", was my reply, but to be perfectly honest I was at a loss.

A few months back, Dallas hosted a Black Arts Festival. The festival was a travelling group of artists with some of the most amazing art I'd ever seen. From booth to booth I wandered as artist after artist showcased their wares. Out of nowhere there was a slight tap on my knee, emanating from a walking cane. As I looked down, an older gentleman peered over a set of glasses, smiled gently, and said, "young man ... I hope you did something special with those pieces I blessed you with." He motioned for me to come closer. I bent down upon which time he whispered, "you know they're valued at over $10,000 now."

Nearly two decades earlier I had visited his home here in Dallas with a mutual friend. Anyone who knows me knows how captivated I am with the black experience in America. From slavery and beyond, nothing holds my attention like that topic. It just so happened that his house was filled with interesting artifacts paying homage to the black struggle. Chains, whips, quilts, posters announcing slave auctions, and so many other incredible items.

While the friend and the artist talked, I drifted from wall to wall, room to room, captivated by what I saw. I picked up this one picture set entitled, "Goree Island: The Middle Passage and asked if I could open it. "By all means" he said. Goree Island, just off the coast of Senegal, is home to the House of Slaves. Some historians believe that as many as 20 million slaves passed through this hellish place before being dispersed to a lifetime of bondage.

The series consisted of 15 incredible pieces that followed the life of an African village. From the time it was raided by slavers all the way up to their being sold at auction upon arriving here in America. One by one I looked at them ... and they looked back at me. What made these pieces even more unique is that he painted them using water from the Atlantic Ocean, while sitting in a slave dungeon.

When I was finished, I neatly placed them back in their folder. As the last one went in, he patted my arm and said, "you take those with you man." I told him thank you, but I remembering thinking thank you doesn't do justice to the amount of gratitude my heart felt at that moment.

A light bulb went off. I had finally found a way to honor that wall. I immediately left the art festival, went home, and grabbed those pictures. I opened the folder and there they were … just as powerful as they were the first time, I saw them. Later that week, I met with a framer to discuss just how I wanted them to be framed. Upon opening the folder, I began telling her what they were. A white woman, she stopped me mid-sentence and said she knew exactly what she was looking at … she'd just never seen it like this. I left them in her care, and she promised she would do them justice.

Around midweek she called. "Done already" I asked. "Not quite" she said. "I just wanted to call and thank you for allowing me to be a part of this incredible experience. In all my years, I have never seen anything like this." I was floored.

A few weeks later she called, this time they were ready, and I eagerly went to retrieve them. True to her word, she did an amazing job. As I said before there were 15 pieces in this set and as a guy who has never been considered handy, I knew I needed a professional to hang them. I called around and found just the guy. We set a date and time. Before he arrived, I positioned the pictures on the floor in the same order I wanted them hung on the wall. He came in and immediately went to work. Banging, screwing, moving his ladder across the floor … and then silence … the kind of silence that told me he was done.

I went in and saw him, standing there looking up in awe. He turned to me, shook my hand, and thanked me. He gathered his tools, cleaned his work area, and turned one last time before leaving and said, "this was the most amazing job I've ever done … thank you again."

That night I sat there for what seemed like forever looking up at those pictures. I had them for years and lived in a house with walls prior to this one, but never got them framed or hung. Then that wall spoke to me yet again. It said, "You never got them framed and hung, because you weren't in a space where you could fully appreciate the blessing."

Some of us have been asking for a blessing. The truth to the matter friend is that every blessing you've ever prayed for is sitting right there in the palm of your hands … You've just got to get a space where you can fully appreciate it.

Finding my way

One of my favorite things to do is going to the mall ... yeah, I know. I love them so much so that when I first moved away from home to Miami, one of the conditions of my stay was that I were given the opportunity to find work in one. The bigger the mall the better the fun, that has always been my motto. What's so crazy about this whole mall thing that I have is that I very rarely purchase anything while I'm there. Even crazier is the fact that while I love malls...I can get lost in them really, really easily.

In Miami whenever I got lost, I'd simply tell whoever was picking me up what store I was at, go stand outside until they arrived. Things got a lot trickier when I moved to Dallas and I was the one doing all the driving. Things got trickier and the malls got a whole lot bigger with some being two, three and four levels high with parking garages to match.

The turning point came in December of 1991 on a trip to the Galleria Mall in far North Dallas. The Galleria is beautiful at any point in the year but in December at Christmas, it's a truly special place to be with an ice rink, a Christmas tree that's close to 6 stories high with decorations abound. I got lost, literally and figuratively and when the mall closed that night it took me an additional hour of wandering through parking garages and lots before I finally found my car.

From that night forward I decided that since I got lost so easily, whenever I found myself in a mall or unfamiliar place, I'd do something really simple; I'd leave a trail. That's right, I'd leave a trail. That way I could easily retrace my steps and find my way back home in a manner of speaking.

The trail can consist of any number of inconspicuous things. A gum wrapper placed in the corner on the floor, a napkin in an obscure location that only I would notice, a cup turned upside down or a subtle mark placed on a wall or pole. No matter what it is, where it's placed or how it looks to anyone else...it always leads me back to home.

What I've found over the years is that this same practice that has worked so well in malls or other places also works well in life. When you find yourself lost or descending into an unfamiliar place make it a point to begin leaving reminders; a trail if you will that leads you back home. A personal victory here, a professional victory there, an accomplished goal here...anything that leads you back to that good place of yours. Anything that leads you back home.

But here's the most important twist; don't just re-trace your steps…go back and re-trace…your words. That's right, re-trace your words. Re-trace your words because contrary to what a lot of people refuse to believe, words really do have power. Chances are that the steps that you took that got you lost or in that place of unfamiliarity…were in fact ordered by the words that you spoke…they were ordered by the words…you spoke…

Leave yourself a trail…

Give yourself reminders…

Find your way back home…

Watch the words you speak…

You'll change the life you live…

The Financial Aid Building

I stopped by my alma mater last week, that's right, the University of Texas at Arlington. Let me tell you—I barely recognized the place. So much has changed, for the better I might add, and it looks and feels like an entirely different campus.

The Business Building where I took most of my classes is still there...but the classrooms have a fresh, new look. There's a new gym that will put any of those high-dollar places we pay monthly fees at to shame!

I stopped by the registrar's office and asked for a schedule for old-time sake only to be told all that's done online now...I had no idea. I wandered around the bookstore—the new bookstore that is and peeked in the library—that now has a Starbucks inside. About the only place that didn't seem touched was the Financial Aid Building. But no matter if they move it, renovate it, or leave it as is, that building will always hold a special meaning for me.

It's where I was taught one of life's most valuable lessons.

Back when I first started classes here, you didn't have to pay upfront. Instead, you were given a date on which your first installment was due. Like so many students at that time, I had applied for and felt certain that I would be receiving financial assistance. But I learned that when it comes to financial assistance and higher education, there are no promises. Weeks passed, and I hadn't heard anything about the status of my assistance package, so I decided to stop by the building to get an update. Surely those funds have been approved by now is what I said to myself.

It was a slow day so there was no line to wait in ... unbelievable I thought to myself. No, they whisked my right back to speak with my counselor—and to my surprise...my application had been denied. A million questions ran through my mind but before I could ask one—a certain peace, a stillness and one of the calmest feelings I've ever felt came over me.

You see, a few weeks earlier, I had received and accepted an incredible job offer. The kind of job that would allow me to pay for my education without any problem while still building a solid foundation from which to live. I zoned out of that conversation with the counselor as she rambled about other options...I think. When she finished, she asked if I had any questions. I said no, thanked her and left.

I didn't have a car yet, so I sat waiting for my ride. While sitting there it dawned on me that all the time I spent filling out paperwork, wasting time, worrying about being approved, wondering how I would pay for this book and that class...only to realize that...all I needed was right there in the palms of my hands...

If you look around there's more than likely an area of your life that you're worrying about. It might not be financial assistance for college—or maybe it is but there's something else ... a friend, a child, a business ... Sometimes, just like I did, we become so fixated on the how...that we forget...the Who. So today, focus on the Who...not the closed door labeled how. Because if He closed that door, rest assured, He's opened another one.

Focus on the Who because when you do, you'll realize that everything you needed...was right there in the palms of your hands...

Miami

As my senior year of high school approached, I thought I had the next phase of my life all figured out. Several colleges were on my wish list including Howard University, Hampton Institute, and Rutgers University. All were a long way from home, but something about that part of the country held and still hold my attention. The year progressed and I began noticing those out-of-state tuition fees, I brought my sights closer to home settling on three others: Bishop College, Prairie View, and The University of Tulsa. Tulsa is my mother's hometown, so I figured if I were going out of state, I'd go to hers.

Every so often, I'd receive information from those three schools, including acceptance letters. Here's where the problem began…I couldn't afford to go. I thought for sure my financial aid packet would get approved, but to my surprise, it was denied. So, there I stood with the summer ending with friends packing up and trending toward the next phase of their lives without a clue as to where mine was headed. I was a man, a young man, without a plan…but I had a plane ticket.

Yes, I had a plane ticket. Earlier that year, my father had purchased a plane ticket for me to visit one of my brothers in Miami. One thing he forgot to tell me – was that it was a one-way ticket. Although I had my heart set on going to one of those schools, he knew that wasn't what I needed…he knew I wasn't ready. About a week into my "visit", I called home to see when I'd be coming back home. That's when he told me of his plan. **His plan was for me to stay in Miami**, enroll in a local community college and ease into this new part of life. I tried and tried to negotiate my return. In the days to follow, friends showed up at his house on my behalf doing the same, but no, he wasn't listening.

So, there I sat in this big, new city in what can best be described as a daze. I finally started righting myself and coming to grips with the reality of the situation. I got a job at the mall and enrolled in school, taking a few basic courses. With more time on my hands, I started running and lifting weights, all day, every single day, and I grew. I grew so much that by the time I came back to his house for a visit, he barely recognized me. That's when it hit me.

Could he have afforded to send me away to any of those schools…probably. It would've been tight – really tight, but he could've managed to make it happen. He could've managed it…but he knew I couldn't. He knew that even though I was 18 and knew right from wrong, how not to be influenced, and was disciplined enough to know when to walk away I still had some growing left. He saw great things in my future, but the old man also knew that too much too soon, would ruin me.

So, he did what good fathers do...he protected his child.

Sometimes we make the greatest plans; foolproof plans in our eyes that just never come to pass because our Father has one that's better. It might not seem like it at the time and you'll undoubtedly be disappointed in the beginning because the ones you had looked so great. But as time goes on and His plans begin to take shape, you'll come to the same realization that I did. You might not agree with it, but when He plans for you, know that He is doing what a good Father does...

He's protecting His child ...

His Voice

I very rarely got into trouble as a child. Oh, trouble was around every corner, but I always knew that if I got into even the least bit of trouble, I had to deal with something much more daunting upon arriving home, my father. With my mother passing so early on he was faced with the task of pretty much raising us on his own and even as a youngster, intuitively, I knew that was a lot to carry. I knew it was so to lighten the load, I did my best to keep my nose clean.

I think the biggest crime I committed in school was chewing gum or being tardy on a couple of occasions but on the whole, my record was pretty much spotless. Around the house my record was just about the same. We were no angels but as kids go, we were fairly tame...most of the time. But on those occasions where he needed to remind us of who was in charge, he raised his voice; making sure his presence was felt.

Over the years, I noticed something though. Yes, he'd raise his voice on that rare occasion when one of us dared to get out of line, and let me tell you, we would listen. But during those times when he really wanted to get his point across, when he really wanted to be heard...he'd say it in a soft voice. He'd say it in a soft voice, a whisper and we knew that no matter what he was saying, listening was in our best interest.

When I got older, I asked him why he often spoke softest when he had the most important things to say. In my mind and in the minds of most, it just seems to make more sense to speak loudly if there was something important to communicate.

He said, "I spoke softly because it forced you guys to focus on me and what I was saying; not the TV, not the schoolbooks, not your little friends outside calling your name...it forced you to focus me and what I was saying. ***Because what I was saying was what mattered the most.***"

You know sometimes the Father will speak to us in a soft, whispering tone but we miss it because we are focusing on this person or that person, this responsibility or that one. We are focusing on everything and everyone else in our lives. From this day forward, spend time focusing on the Father and what He has to say. Block out all of the distractions for a time so that you can hear the soft, soothing whispers that can only come from above. Focus on the Father and what He has to say...because His say is the say that matters the most.

That Race

One of my greatest regrets is not having children as I've always wanted to be a father. People tell me there's still time and I'm hopeful so hey, you never know but to date, no one's calling me Daddy. But even though I don't have any children of my own, I've mentored several in my area and those opportunities have been rewarding. Through it all, they grew, and you know what...so did I.

A couple of weeks ago, one of those young men called me in need of a favor. He was moving into his second apartment and all those great friends he made over the course of the years were nowhere to be found. Isn't it amazing how on moving day friends just disappear? So, since he couldn't find any of those "great" friends to help him move, he called me. No worries I told him, I'm on my way.

I pulled into his complex and there he was standing next to the truck he borrowed—with two large sofas waiting upstairs for us to move. Now, here's where things got interesting. The sofas had to be moved—all the way down from apartment...on the 3rd floor. From there, they had to be moved all the way up to the 3rd floor at his new place. No big deal I thought. He works out and so do I, so we'll knock this out in no time at all.

We grabbed the first sofa and began our trek. We made it up the first flight of stairs. He paused and asked if we could rest. "Sure", I told him. About two minutes passed and we moved up the next flight where he asked for another break. "No problem", I said. We finally made it up to the truck, but before going back up to get the other sofa, he asked if we could rest for a minute, "Sure" was my response...then he asked me why I wasn't breathing hard or tired.

He laughed and said, "Oh yeah; I forgot you ran a marathon, this ain't nothing for you." I smiled back and thought to myself, ***"Yeah...I did that ..."***

It's funny how now when life throws a curve ball or something unexpected my way...I come back to the marathon I ran; I come back to that race. Have I walked through life since that time, oblivious to the challenges and impervious to pain—not at all. But because I ran that race...I'm convinced there isn't one I can't finish.

You may never lace up your shoes to run a marathon, but in all our lives there's "that race." That race may have been your being a single mother or single father. That race may have been your working two jobs, or maybe three to make ends meet. That race, the one that defined you may have been night school, beating cancer, or surviving the loss of a loved one. You're still standing...you crossed the finish line...you made it.

So, when things get tough and you feel as though you can't make it...remember that race...

Yeah...you did that...

The Power of When

I was a good kid; so good that I only got three spankings in my entire life. Of the three, the first, and most memorable came at the hands of my mother. I was 4 at the time and while she sat up front watching her soaps, I was in the back jumping off the bed, having a ball and making a ton of noise.

I'd scale the bed...jump off...BOOM...and break out into raucous laughter. Time and time again I repeated this and then out of nowhere, her voice pierced the fun.

"If I have to come back there", she said. I stopped for a minute before starting again. Then out of nowhere, her voice said, "Little boy...if you make me get out of this chair ..." I paused...but before long I was back at it, jumping off that bed, landing hard on that floor but having the best time doing it.

"Son...if you make me say your name one more time ..." Once again, I put my fun on hold before giving in to temptation, climbing that bed and jumping off...BOOM! BOOM!

That's when she lost it...*" **Lynn...when I get back there ...**"* and that's when everything, I mean everything changed...

You see, even as a 4-year-old kid, I could tell there was a huge difference between the words if and when. If meant there was a small chance of her coming back to see me, but it wasn't a certainty. WHEN on the other hand; when meant she was on her way and it was just a matter of time. If meant her coming back was a possibility, but not a promise...WHEN meant her coming back there had become a reality...a guarantee.

$$ \text{🌲 🌲 🌲} $$

I and F; two letters but when you put them together, they become one of the most powerful words in the dictionary. Hey, you ever wonder what you could accomplish by replacing if, with when? Instead of if I could just find a way to lose those last 10 pounds...it becomes when I find a way to lose those last 10 pounds. Instead of if I could just get that promotion, it becomes when I get that promotion. Instead of if I could get the courage to start my own business it becomes when I start my own business.

As we start another day, in honor of mothers across the world including yours, replace the word if with when because when you do possibilities become realities and...everything...I mean everything will change...

Donuts

Over the years, my father has imparted a great deal of wisdom and with each passing year, it comes to mean so much more. There was the time I bought my first car and came home to take him for a spin and out of nowhere another car went speeding past us. He tapped me and said watch this...about 20 seconds later we sat at a red light...right next to that car that had sped past us. He smiled and said those folks who are always in a hurry will not get there any faster than the rest of us; slow down.

He taught me about good stuff— jazz. Gillespie, Coltrane, Miles, Parker, if you can name it, chances are I've heard it. I bought him some good stuff for Father's Day this year. During one of our most recent conversations he went on and on about how he had broken his favorite album. I listened, went out and found that album and gave it to him. I think I got a bigger kick out of him getting it than he did.

I learned how to fight by watching him...not in a boxing ring, just in day-to-day life. Raising five boys and one girl after losing the love of your life—that's a fight—but he never backed down; he fought. Being diagnosed with Stage 4 Colon cancer in October and all but being counted out as his body withered away to 106 pounds required a fighter. Yesterday when I saw him, he proudly announced that he was cancer-free (I heard him the first 1,000 times) and now weighs 172 pounds. Yeah...he fought.

"If you take care of what you got, what you got will take care of you" ...is one of his favorite truisms. Back in 1998, I bought a brand spanking new truck and each time the maintenance was due...I remembered him saying that, so I took care of that truck. I got nearly 400,000 miles out of it...I guess you could say it took care of me too.

One of the most precious morsels of wisdom he gave me took place, believe it or not...over a donut. Growing up donuts, specifically glazed twists were my thing and if you had a glazed twist, I instantly became your #1 fan. We didn't get donuts often but when we did, it felt like heaven and each time they arrived, everyone knew the twists were reserved for me. We didn't get them often, but Saturdays were the days when we were most likely to see that big, friendly white box sitting on our kitchen table.

One Saturday morning I came bounding down the hallway as he announced his arrival, with donuts. I opened the box but to my surprise, someone had taken the glazed twist! Someone had taken the donut, THE DONUT that was reserved for me! I was only 6 and to me, the world was about to end...until my father calmly pulled me close and changed my perspective.

He pulled that big white box down off the table and told me to look at all of those other donuts still in there, still waiting to be eaten...made of the same dough, with the same glazed icing, made in the same oven, in the same store. So, I dug in and ate a bunch of those other ones and smiled with satisfaction after the last bite, realizing that they were, in fact, the same...

They just looked different...

🌲 🌲 🌲

At the crack of dawn on Father's Day, phones ring all over the country at the same time, big breakfast, lunch, brunch, and dinner feasts are prepared. All these things are done in honor of those incredible men we call father. We laud him, fawn over him even as he stands 10 feet tall in our eyes, sometimes taller. With each glance or thought we're touched by something he has said or done. We give him neckties, watches, socks, suits to match those ties, hats, colognes; you name it, chances are he, the father gets it.

That was yesterday. Today he's back to being 6 feet tall, maybe shorter with hair that's graying at the temples or gone, wearing a uniform adorned with a patch that has his name on it, in boots or a well-worn suit...but please remember...he's still the same incredible guy... made of the same things he was the day before ...

He just looks different...

We did it!

My first two years of college were spent at junior colleges; first in Miami and then in Dallas. Going to college, even a junior college, was a transition for me, filled with a totally different set of life challenges. Looking back, I think I managed them all pretty well and actually made the Dean's List both years. After accumulating well over 60 credit hours, I was ready to move on to a major university. I was turned down by my first two choices, so I enrolled at the University of Texas at Arlington. Now, when I arrived, let me tell you, I walked into the classroom thinking that I would have the same types of success as I had in junior college...but it didn't quite work out that way. A's turned to C's and the elation I used to feel whenever an assignment was returned in junior college quickly turned to frustration on the university level.

One night after receiving another C (which had unfortunately become my norm) I took the long route home and decided college wasn't for me. I came in and angrily told my sister of my decision to forego college and just work. She patiently listened to every reason I gave her for quitting and then calmly addressed each one. At the end she dismissed me and said, "No; "We" are not going to quit." The next morning before leaving for work I tried to make my case one more time but once again, she was hearing none of it.

That evening when I arrived home from class, she was nowhere to be found – but dinner was on the stove. To my room I went to drop off my bookbag and I noticed my clothes had been folded and put away. A fresh scent called me to my bathroom and upon turning on the lights I saw it had been scrubbed from top to bottom.

I figured this would go on for a month or so, but I was wrong. For the next three years no matter how late I came in, there was always dinner waiting. No matter how early I left for work, there was always something for breakfast. No matter how dirty my clothes got at work that week, she was always there to clean them. Rent, light, phone, cable...I never wrote a check for any of those. She'd pay them, tell me the amounts I owed and on payday, I'd deposit those amounts into her account. I financed my entire education and around registration, money was tight – I mean really tight. No worries, because during those times, she'd put a little extra toward the household bills, leaving me room to breathe ... and live.

🌲 🌲 🌲

As I stood in line at the Registrar's office during the final days prior to graduation, I thought about all of those times. I especially remembered the conversation where she told me that "We" were not going to quit. She never came into the classroom with me...but I would've never made it out of the classroom without her. I got the diploma...but "We" did it.

I went on to graduate school and got my MBA. Prior to the commencement ceremony, I approached the Dean, asking if he'd allow my sister to escort me across the stage that night as I received my diploma. He said he didn't see any problem and with that, we made plans to make that walk together. By this time, I was living on my own and doing for myself, but I realized if she hadn't been there to do for me when I couldn't do for myself, none of this would be happening.

As we sat in the stands waiting for my row to be called up, I told her thanks for being there. She said, "It's what Mom would have expected." She smiled and said, "she left but I feel like she is still right here with us." We walked across the stage, got the diploma, and got back to our seats. I took off my cap, unzipped my gown, reached into the left pocket of my suit jacket, and pulled out a picture of my Mom, the one I always carry on special occasions. I nudged my sister, showed her the picture, smiled, and said, "she is." And then that's when I realized that in my mind, it was just me and her; that was the "We" I was thinking of. But in my sister's mind, it was me, her, and Mom...that was the "WE" she was speaking of.

As that day turned to night, we laughed and reflected...but most of all we smiled, two of us in body and mind and one of us in spirit, surrounded by family... remembering how no matter what life threw our way...

We did it!

Phyllis Hyman

They don't make R&B music like they used to. I know...I know there are some who will disagree because good music is a relative phrase. But from my perspective there just isn't a lot of it out there anymore. Oh, but there was a day when the R&B world was filled with some beautiful sounds and a lot of it was being made by women.

You had Anita Baker, Chaka Khan, Cherelle, Regina Belle and no list is complete without the late, great Whitney Houston. And while I loved and still love all those women and the music they made and make...none of them, at least not in my mind, could touch Phyllis Hyman.

While she never received the notoriety of any of her contemporaries, Phyllis Hyman was arguably the most talented female voice of her time. This past weekend with the college football schedule being sparse, I had a little, make that a lot of time on my hands. So instead of sitting around watching television I popped in a couple of her CDs...and got re-acquainted with some good music. Although her music was and still is beautiful, there was hurt in just about every lyric she sung.

Following her suicide in 1995 I remember watching a special documenting her music, life, and the challenges she faced in the industry. I'll never forget the comment that one female entertainment reporter made. She simply said, "We spent so much time hearing her music, but we never took the time to listen because if we had listened, we would have heard her pain. And it would have made all the difference."

Starting today don't just hear...listen. When you're talking to a co-worker overreacting over something that should not even bring a reaction...listen. When dealing with a spouse or loved one and you hear something "different", stop hearing and start listening. If you hear something disturbing from a child, listen...there's more to it, they need you.

Listen because listening means love. Listening means you matter. Listening means I care...and listening, can make all the difference.

Waiting on the snow

One of my biggest disappointments with the winter of 2019 is we didn't get a single snowflake. Not one. In fact, I don't even remember the local weathermen hinting at the chance of snow. I know, I know, how did this Texas guy gain such an affinity for the harsh weather conditions? Not sure myself, but there's something about that type of weather that really resonates with me. Whereas most people I know crave tropical environments for vacation, I on the other hand crave a getaway that requires hats, gloves, and a layer of clothing – or two! While we didn't get snow that year, I vividly remember my first snow experience. The night before it happened, my mother tucked me in and promised she'd have a surprise for me at breakfast. Back then, food didn't do a thing for me, so I figured it'd be a toy of some sort.

That morning, she came in, grabbed my little hand, led me to the front, opened the door and there it was ... snow! I couldn't get dressed fast enough! For the next two days, friends and family from all over the neighborhood, built snowmen and snow angels, threw snowballs, and simply stood in awe of this incredible act of nature.

As the temperature began to rise, our fun started to fade and the snow that brought us so much joy, slowly began to melt. The chill was still in the air, but there wasn't enough of a chill to sustain the magic. This made me sad and that night, I found my way to the big sliding glass door in the back of our house, looking up, hoping it would snow again. No one else, just me.

As the youngest in the house, my mother always kept close tabs on me. She came looking and found me sitting there and in her sweet voice asked, "what you doing?" "Waiting on the snow", I replied. *"**I'll wait with you**",* and with that she plopped down next to me. There we sat for a good little while – me waiting on snow, her conversing with her little boy as he waited...

We talked about the blue jacket and matching blue gloves I loved so much... riding my bike without training wheels and learning how to comb my hair. Our time together was so brief, and my father often says this is why memories of her burn so intensely within me. We talked and talked some more, but the next thing I knew, I was waking up in bed. I opened the shades, looked outside, and realized that snow never showed up ... but I was so happy my mother did...

As the years have gone by, I've stood at that place in our old house many times. The door has changed, and my father has actually moved out, but a change of address can never erase that special memory. Me waiting on the snow, her knowing it would never come, but waiting with me just the same. Waiting, just the same in a way only a mother could.

Take a moment and go back to that place in your life where you wanted something, someone, or something to happen. In certain situations, your boys, your girls, your best friends are there. Then there are those times when no one else showed up – those times you were waiting on the snow.

The silence was pierced by the sweet voice of your mother. Isn't it amazing how she can always find you during those times? She listened, you talked, she listened, you talked, she loved, you grew. Before you knew it, you were in the most peaceful place life has to offer. You'll smile, your heart will too as you realize, that snow … it never showed up … but remember how happy you were …

Because your mother did…

What Love Looks Like

I used to think my father was just a mean old man. All his rules, be home by this time, do this, don't do that...I said no. Yeah, in my mind he was crazy...hateful. But now, oh my...I spent this past Thursday afternoon with him and the more we talked, the more all those things he used to say way back when came rushing back to me...Things like...

Always love your mother...and don't waste time with anyone who doesn't: He has this saying; it goes like this, ***"If God made anything more beautiful than a mother, He kept it up there in Heaven for Himself."*** Mothers, they're so special; yes, they are, and God misses them so much that from time to time, He calls them back home. You never know when yours will get that call...so don't waste time with those who don't understand how special, how sacred, how things I can't even put into words, their mother is. More importantly, don't waste time not loving yours.

Put the trash out and lock up: When I was a teen it was my responsibility to lock the house up at night but before I did, I had to put the trash was out. I remember a time or two I forgot and in that small frame house of ours, the stench from the day before is how the new day began. It wasn't a good feeling. Hey sometimes you'll have a trashy day on the inside but don't make the mistake of taking with you into tomorrow. If you have a bad day, before going to bed, get over it...lock up your mind, lock up your heart...and put that trash out!

Eat right: Growing up I hated all vegetables and most fruits, but he forced me to eat them all. He always ate his which explains why he gets along better than people half his age. I do better now and last week, he encouraged me to keep eating good foods, and be sure I'm thinking good thoughts. Because good or bad, whatever you put inside, food or thoughts, is going to show up on the outside.

Don't you speed up: I remember the first time he rode in a car with me. We were riding along and out of nowhere a sports car blew by us! My first impulse was to speed up to try and catch it but before I could, he tapped me on my knee and said, "Hey don't you speed up, keep going at your pace; you'll end up right there with him...and maybe ahead." A few minutes later...I looked to my left and that car was right there. Eventually we ended up passing that car, just like he said we might. Sometimes you'll look at what so and so is doing or what they got and wonder why you don't. Your first impulse will be to speed up. Do yourself a favor...don't do that. Just keep moving at your pace...eventually you'll catch up...you might even pass them...

Run: When my mother passed, my father was working three jobs and looking for a fourth. It wasn't for money, he needed something to keep his mind off the fact that he lost the love of his life. One day, there were no more shifts to work, no more clocks to punch, no more jobs to go to...so in his slack's and wingtips, he took off running. He took off running and said it was the best feeling he'd ever felt. He's been running ever since. Running cleared his mind, it gave him a purpose; it gave him the peace that he needed to keep going. I'm not saying that you need to become a runner; not literally anyway. But you're never going to get to where you want to go by just sitting there. Try running.

Run some more: There were days when he used to run and the answers, the reasons why, the peace that he was seeking came after a short run. Then there were those days when it called for him to run a little further...run some more as he likes to say. When you feel the urge to run some more, that's not your trainer or your diet plan calling you; that's the answer, the why, the peace you're seeking so don't stop: run some more.

God really is listening, and you should be too: "You pray every morning and night and you don't need to use all of them big words just talk", is what he always says when we talk about prayer. Just talk because He listens and not only is He listening...He answers, so make sure you're listening.

Those are not friends, those are associates: "One of your associates is at the door." Associates...no, that's my friend I thought but he saw differently...now I do too. Over the course of time, the volume of traffic at my door has dropped. Some people, associates if you will, have come and gone...but my real friends keep coming by. The longer you live the more obvious the difference between a friend and an associate will become. Hold onto those friends...make memories with and cherish them...they're gifts.

All those lessons and so many more...that was wisdom he was passing along. He knew how much we'd miss my mother...and he also knew we'd never understand how others could mistreat theirs. My old man understood that with all we'd been through our minds would be susceptible to a lot of negative stuff...trash...so he wanted us to think good thoughts to keep us standing tall. He understood that others had a head start because we lost so much in one day. But he also knew that if we tried to keep up, we never could but if we kept going, we would catch up and even pass some. He was right. There were days I know I wanted to stop running...but I ran some more. I found out that God really does listen...and He talks back, and I know who my friends are too.

Growing up if you ever thought your parents were crazy...they were just crazy about you.

If you felt as though they were ever being hateful...it's only because they cared.
And if you thought they were being mean...all they were really doing was saying ...

I love you...

Fred Hampton

Well, it's finally here. What is it you ask…"it", is The Black Panther, the most highly anticipated movie in years! Advance ticket sales have been incredible with fans from all over logging in and showing up to get theirs. The cool thing about it is that even though The Black Panther is a black superhero, it hasn't just been black fans who've been purchasing the tickets. Brown fans, yellow fans, red fans, and white fans have all been making plans to see The Black Panther. It's interesting, refreshing even to see all these different ethnicities getting so excited…but it's not the first time it happened.

Back in the 1960's there was another Black Panther…he also brought a crowd.

***

Tired of being harassed, bullied, and mistreated by the police, The Black Panther Party for Self Defense was formed in 1966. When the party first began, they barely registered a blip on the national radar but at their apex…J. Edgar Hoover himself labeled them, "the greatest threat to internal security in the United States/"

The Panthers, as they came to be called, weren't afraid of anyone or anything. They carried sticks, knives, and guns: real big guns, but the most effective tool in their arsenal was the spoken word…and no one spoke words better than Fred Hampton.

Huey Newton and Bobby Seale founded the party but during the height of the movement, the bulk of their lives were spent in prison and mired in various legal battles. Malcolm X had already been assassinated and MLK's days were numbered so no worries there -- those situations were well in hand. But when the FBI heard Fred Hampton speak, they realized their greatest fear had become a reality…a Black Messiah was on the horizon. So, after hearing him they set the wheels of death in motion and on the morning of December 4th, 1969, the Chicago Police raided his apartment and murdered him.

Was he slain because he carried a gun? It wasn't that because he understood the gun laws better than those who wrote them so if he were carrying one, he did so within the limits of the day. He wasn't running drugs, sticking folks up, jacking cars, or peddling women, no sir, no ma'am. His gift and his curse, his crime if you will was his ability to connect people.

When Fred Hampton spoke, yellow people felt loved, not tolerated. When he spoke, brown people couldn't take their eyes off him, he gave them hope. When he opened his mouth, white people stopped, and said what if and when he was in the presence of blacks and began to orate, dreams slowly took the form of realities. His voice was that powerful but to some, power is a threat so his had to be silenced. But even in silence, Fred Hampton can still be heard.

So, if you're in attendance this weekend, before leaving your theatre, stop for a minute and remember Fred Hampton. They took his voice, but you still have yours so open your mouth and say a solemn thank you to The Black Messiah who never was, killed because his words rang too true, laid down his life at the tender age of 21 while standing tall for his people.

That Black Panther...was a real superhero!

Call your Mother

When you lose a mother, that's a different type of loss altogether. Nothing compares to it—and there are days when the loss can feel as new as the day it happened. The calendar says the distance should've allowed healing but ask anyone who's ever experienced it and they'll tell you the wound always stays fresh.

Last year, I found myself in a situation, not knowing which way to go. I stopped and said aloud, "I'll just call mom" … Only to realize, I haven't been able to make that call for a very long time. That's what a mother's love does. Even when she's gone, there's a sense of nearness that never subsides. I couldn't call her with my phone, so I called her with my heart. As always, she picked up on the first ring and the response she gave, made everything just right.

When your mother leaves, sounds, tastes, looks, feels---things only a mother can give become forever scorched into your heart so softly that you never even felt the burn. As I've cycled through the seasons of this loss, valuable lessons continue to reveal themselves.

One winter afternoon, I came running into the house—hurt and angry. An older kid, one of the big kids as we used to call them wouldn't let me play, have my way or something or another. So off to tell my mother I went. Mothers back then were the judge, jury and executioner and I knew with her on my side, the tables would turn.

She met me at the door and I immediately began pleading my case...but I stopped, when I noticed her face, fighting to hold back a smile. I began again, this time with all the passion my little heart could muster, reliving the painful details of the event, but again, I noticed her smile. I paused...and with no further warning, she burst into laughter and with that, I had no choice but to do the same.

I remember a lot about that day. I remember the blue coat with yellow trim I wore and the navy gloves that fit snuggly on my little hands. I'll never forget the way the sun seemingly stood watch in the sky, giving off just the right amount of heat to make the cold day warm enough to enjoy. I can still smell dinner cooking on the stove and I also hear the game show sounds emanating from the television that sat just off to the right.

All those years later, all those things and a few others have remained with me. But what I remember most is that when I came running in, my whole world was crumbling around me – ***all it took was a smile from my mother to put it back together again.***

Life doesn't always go as planned. You stay late, arrive early, work weekends and prep for a promotion, but life offers a pink slip. He or she is the one; yes, they do it for you, but every year at that special time of the year, you find yourself alone. Children are growing like weeds and so too are your hopes for them. For some reason, they can't seem to see the vast amount of potential their lives hold, or the dangers lurking on the other side. All are part of the cycle of life – all are times when a conversation with your mother would make everything just right. I've seen it, on grown, hardened men with an edge so sharp it could cut through diamonds. But when they got tired, when they couldn't cut anymore, they turned to their mother, and her smile, helped finish the job.

Life won't always go as planned. Those times when it doesn't, pick up the phone and call your mother. For those of us who can't, pick up your heart and dial her number...she'll answer on the first ring. Your world might be crumbling around you, but when you hear her smile...

It'll put it all back together again.

Gordon

Just like everyone else these days I have a GPS system in my car. Mine works like a charm most of the time but there are those instances where it tends to go a little haywire and just make stuff up. The real problem isn't with the GPS system, it's with the owner. That's right, me, the owner; too cheap to buy an updated version of the software so from time to time the route becomes adventurous to say the least. Adventurous and frustrating to the point where I almost want to throw up my hands, turn back and go home. But then I stop and remember why I came in the first place and the "why" of it all pushes me to keep going.

In March of 1863 Gordon, a slave from the brutal slave state Louisiana bravely made his escape. Having tried many times before and failed Gordon was all too familiar with the consequences should he be caught this time...but this time, he had a plan. Back then bounty hunters, overseers and slave catchers employed well-trained hunting dogs to track and, in most cases, capture runaways. All these dogs needed were the slightest whiff of a slave and off they went, stalking their prey. Without question the most horrifying sound a runaway slave could hear was the baying of a pack of dogs, announcing that they were on his or her tail. This usually meant that it was only a matter of time before they were caught, returned to the plantation, and severely punished. But this time, Gordon had a plan.

He trudged through swamps and rivers and when he emerged, he rubbed himself all over with onions with the hopes of throwing the pursuing dogs off of his scent. The plan worked like a charm and in April of 1863, Gordon arrived in a Union camp, announcing himself as a free man of color, ready to fight for those that still remained in bondage. The Union officers welcomed him with open arms and asked that he submit to a full physical to which Gordon eagerly complied. When he took off his shirt and exposed his back...the entire camp fell silent. His back, filled with gruesome scars, gave Union soldiers who up until that time had only heard of what occurs on plantations an up-close and personal look at the horrors of slavery. Pictures were taken and circulated amongst abolitionists and the mangled back of Gordon became known as the Map of Slavery. When abolitionists saw this, it gave them a renewed sense of purpose and energized their drive to eradicate slavery in America.

The picture was also sent to Union camps throughout the nation only this time with a different caption consisting of three simple words; "Why We Fight." You see up until that time some Union soldiers were unclear as to why they were engaged in this civil war. Oh yes, they knew that holding slaves in the South was wrong, but it wasn't touching them. But once they saw this photo, they like those abolitionists gained a different perspective on their mission. They, black and white, fought harder, dug deeper, resolved to not quit until the monster that was slavery met death. They gained perspective because now...they had a "why."

Raise your hand if you have ever been in a position where you just wanted to throw in the towel, quit and move on. A lot of hands went up and most of us probably have taken that easy way out at some point. But the next time you get to that fork in the road, stop for a minute...remember the "why." You enrolled in school for a better life, that's why...don't quit. You fell in love because you were made for one another, that's why...don't quit. You started this health journey with the goal of becoming better; for yourself...don't quit.

You were called to be so much more than what you have settled for being in the past so whenever quitting comes to your door, before answering it, before giving up...stop for a moment...

And remember why you fight...

I AM WHO I AM

All the books of the Bible are fascinating reads and one of my favorites is the Book of Exodus. Exodus tells the story of the children of Israel leaving slavery, led by the prophet Moses. Before Moses accepted the assignment of leading God's chosen people out of Egypt, it required a little convincing. Unsure he would be listened to, Moses asked God who he should say sent him when the Israelites asked. God responded by saying…" Tell them I AM WHO I AM" …and their conversation ended … that's pretty awesome…That line has a lot of meaning to me.

When I first went away to college, I enrolled at Miami Dade Community College in Miami, Florida. A community college yes, but the campus I attended had the third largest student population of any college in America trailing only The University of Michigan and Texas A&M University. I remember that first day of class like it were yesterday. I was one of the first to enter, but as time went by, more students filed into that amphitheater setting. Before long, every seat was taken, filled with a young person eager to take this all-important next step on life's journey.

The class filled up and the instructor walked in and from the start … she told us she was different, and she was. With long blonde hair, makeup that can only be described as creative and a jam box in tow … she was different indeed. Instead of just calling the roll and students responding with, "here", she required the student stand and introduce themselves, including major and where they were from. I watched and watched as one by one, student after student rose to their feet and followed protocol. Then my time came … and man, was I nervous. Being in front of a group who from the looks of things knew one another but didn't know me was a scary proposition.

My name was called I stood, announced my major and then said, ***"I'm from Killeen."*** Students from every which way turned and said, "You went to Killeen?" I said, "Yes" …emboldened by the fact that everyone seemed to have heard of my hometown. They started asking if I knew this person and that person and none of them sounded familiar. That's when the professor, a transplant from Austin, stepped in and solved the riddle. She knew I meant Killeen, Texas but the other students in the classroom thought I meant Miami Killian High School…same pronunciation but different spellings. Miami Killian, at the time, was considered the "it" high school in Miami. While my classmates cooled toward my introduction as they found out I wasn't from Killian…I saw it as an opportunity to show how proud I was to be from … Killeen.

I told them about Fort Hood, the largest military installation in the world that borders Killeen. I gushed about my neighborhood, Marlboro Heights, telling how it was the embodiment of the word community. From there I spoke about the war veterans who proudly called Killeen home and how equally proud we are to call them ours. In essence…I told them I AM WHO I AM and while they might have wanted me to be from Killian...I'm from Killeen...and in my mind, that's pretty awesome...

Hey, at some point, do yourself a favor and have an "I AM WHO I AM" moment. Remember where you came from, no matter if the population is 200 or 2 million; take pride in it. Remember who you come from; they might not have been perfect, but you made it, remember that. Look at all the relationships you built along the way, even the ones that hurt; cherish them. Think about all those special people, places and things that have helped to make you and then boldly, freely say, "I AM WHO I AM" ...because when you do, you'll begin to realize...

You're pretty awesome...

That Great Big Wall

In early 2018, the stock market realized one of its biggest losses in history, falling a record 1600 points in one day. To put that in perspective, if you had invested $1000 on Friday, Monday that investment would have only been worth $920. Since that time, investors near and far, old, and new, have been reviewing their portfolios and strategically making decisions to recoup those lost assets. Amazing isn't it? And while those losses were tremendous...the greatest losses that the market has ever seen...

Were lives...

In the 1700's when America was a loosely knit group of colonies trying desperately to find her way, slavery was alive and well in the north. History most often tells us that slavery was a southern institution but while it flourished in the south, its roots were in the north. As young America fought to free herself from English rule, colonists fought violent Indian war parties here at home. Nowhere was this fight fought more heavily than what is now known as New York City.

Slave owners who were also viewed as the community leaders of their time found themselves in a quandary. By day they would build the city...but by night the Indians would tear it down. One street was especially important as it was the central location where business was transacted and without it, their efforts were doomed. So, these leaders hatched a plan that called for black slaves to build a protective wall around this street. Job well done as usual and over the course of time, the raids lessened, and a city began to blossom.

More time passed and this street became the preferred location for slave auctions. The wall was used to hide the wretched, sorrowful scenes of families being sold and torn apart. Fathers to never see their wives again... Mothers to never see their children again... Families to never be families again.... The street needed a name and with all of the walls that were built in and around it, it became known as...***Wall Street***...the street that stands as the central nerve of today's global economy.

You can't take a step on what is arguably the most famous street in the world without being touched by the contributions of the African American, and one day soon, I'm going there. And when I arrive, I won't be running to hear the opening bell or to watch the frenzied activity on the trading floor. I 'll do like so many have done before me, choosing instead to utter a soft thank you to those brave souls who passed that way. Thank you because each of us represents one of them who stood on the auction block and although they were bound, we are living proof that they couldn't be broken. And because they refused to be broken...because as the song says, they made it there...brother, sister...you and I, regardless of what anyone wants us to believe,

We can make it anywhere...

The Overflow

Lunch-shaming is happening all over the country as districts grapple with unpaid lunch debt brought on by families unable to pay for school meals. The thought of a child not eating saddens my heart. It also warms my heart while bringing me back to a valuable life lesson.

As a kindergartener, we didn't get lunch, because by the time lunch rolled around, we were on our way home. We didn't get a lunch period, but we did get that one thing that makes five-year old kids around the world light up...snack time! Each day my mom would pack me the same things: a thermos of milk, two Ding Dong Cakes and a bag of Frito's. Every single day that year without fail whenever I opened my lunch box those four things would be waiting for me.

Now, that's a whole lot for a little kid; especially a little kid who didn't like to eat. When the year first began, I'd eat it all but over course of time I began to come home with a lunch box that was half full. I'd look at her and apologetically say, "It was too much, mom." Each time she would cup my face and chuckle.

What I didn't know was that a lot of the kids at the school I went were from families that couldn't afford to pack a snack. We weren't one of those families. No, at our house my mom made sure we had breakfast, lunches, dinners, and snacks galore...I guess you might say we had an overflow.

One afternoon after delivering the news that I had failed to finish lunch yet again, she cupped my little face as usual, chuckled, and struck her best, "I have a bright idea" pose. She said, ***"Tell you what baby, whenever you have too much, let's just share it with someone else..."***

In this life, you won't always be down but by the same token, you won't always be up either. There'll be times when you might not know where your next meal is going to come from, how this bill is going to be paid or look around and realize that your take home pay simply isn't taking you home anymore. Then there'll be times when you have all those things taken care of and then some...those times when you find yourself living in...the overflow. An overflow...bringing some home at the end of each day because, "it was too much."

When you find yourself in those times rather than just holding onto it all, stop and remember that there are plenty more in the house those blessings came from, blessings galore.

More importantly, stop and remember that when you're in that place and time where you have too much, an overflow...know that it wasn't all meant for you...

It was sent and meant...to be shared with someone else...

God's Eyes

Whenever I go home nowadays, I struggle to find any of my friends. Whereas it used to be a common occurrence to bump into one, those times are now few and far in between. Even during the holidays it's hard to find an old face. I miss those days, times, and people. The struggle is even harder now as my father has moved out of the old neighborhood. But even when he was there, some of those parents who had become friends, pillars of a lifetime, pieces of our hearts were slowly but surely being called home to Heaven.

It's hard to catch up with old faces so when I'm home, I spend time with old places. My father moved but as fate would have it, he moved right around the corner from my old elementary school...one of my favorite old places. A few weeks back before heading home, I pulled up on the parking lot of that old place...that old friend. The memories started to flood to the point where I literally drifted back in time...

My first stop...I had to do it—was the kindergarten wing. I started thinking back to that first day of school, that first day away from home...From there, I went over to the playground and looked at the swing set and thought back to how big and imposing it once was. Back in those days, it looked like a ride out of an amusement park. The same could be said for the slide and merry-go-round.

Back then, they looked so frightening and I remember always approaching them with fear and trepidation... But when I came back on this visit...everything seemed so small and I wasn't cautious, frightened or the least bit afraid.

The sidewalk used to take forever to get from one end to the next even when I was running my fastest...now only required a few good strides. The fence that I used to get in trouble for climbing because it was so, so high...I can step over it now...

I stood flat-footed and touched the top of the apparatus that held the swing set together. Yeah, that swing set that once doubled as a monster...yeah, that one. I laid on the slide that once seemed to go on forever and my feet hung off it; I was too big. That merry-go-round that used to take the entire kindergarten class to push...with one good push from me it spun around for several minutes. All those things that once looked so big and presented such a challenge way back when now seemed so small in my eyes...

No big deal.

God views the challenges in our lives the same way. Financial, personal, and professional challenges that we see as too big, He sees them as so small...

As we start another day remember what we face and our perspective of them changes as we grow older. But it's good to know that we serve a God whose perspective never changes; a God who looks at every challenge we are or will be confronted with today and in the days that are to come and simply says...

No big deal...

Johnnie Marable

Time was when I was the fastest little kid on my block. Didn't matter what their first or last name was, the military rank of their father or ethnicity; any kid you brought my way would leave with an L on their record...until this one kid moved in a few doors down. He was not your average kid. He was big for his age, tall with long arms, long legs...and he was fast. He was the kind of fast that had me worried to be honest as I realized my title as the fastest kid on the block was in serious jeopardy.

The day finally came for our much anticipated (about as anticipated as 7 or 8 years old can have) showdown in one of our impromptu neighborhood track meets. He beat me the first race. No problem I thought I'll just get him in the second one, but he was having none of that as he beat me in that one too. The third and fourth races came around and the results were no different: him first, me second.

As we approached the fifth one, I was a little, make that a lot rattled. My title had been stripped...a new king had been crowned. We got in position and this kid, big for his age, tall with long arms, long legs and fast could see the disappointment on my face. So, before the race began, he nudged me and whispered, "You take first...I'll take second." My heart leapt for joy as I was able to regain a small measure of honor back.

We became really good friends and years later he reminded me of that day he made that incredibly selfless gesture during a walk home from football practice. He went on and on and on and then looked down at me and asked if I remembered...to which I smugly replied, ***"No; sorry but I don't remember!"*** Oh, sure I remembered, how could I forget? But I figured what the heck, why not have a little fun?

Before entering our neighborhood, we had to cross a busy highway. Crossing that highway meant we were home but crossing highways -- crossing streets, was something I wasn't good at. This big friend knew this and kind of acted as my unofficial crossing guard. So, we walked along and got to the highway and then out of nowhere he bolted across, leaving me on the other side. I looked over at him...confused. He looked back over at me...smiling...laughing and shouted ..."do you remember now?"

"Good one", I yelled hoping this would be enough for him to come rescue his boy but after about 2 minutes it became obvious that he wasn't coming back to get me. I finally got up the courage to make it over to the other side and when I did, I let him have it, screaming, pointing, gesturing...before we both fell out laughing.

As we parted ways, he called my name and calmly said, "Hey man while you were over there doing all that worrying, I never left you. I was watching and waiting on the other side and I wasn't going to let anything happen to you man."

This kid who was big for his age, tall with long arms, long legs and fast crossed over to the other side a few years back. He's home now. But rest assured he's watching, he's waiting. I worry, I hurt but, I understand that the kind of guy he was...he's not going to let anything happen to me....

RIP old friend...

I'll always remember...

Your Inside Voice

There was a time when I could name every teacher, every single one I ever had from elementary school all the way through high school. I could rattle their names of like it was nothing with the grade, the grades that I made and what I liked best about each of them. Well, sad to say that time has come and gone as now I can only remember a handful but one teacher, I'll never forget is my 1st Grade teacher...Mrs. Nelson. Mrs. Nelson was a brilliant woman whose mere presence was enough to make a group of six-year-olds like us fall in line.

She didn't stand for any nonsense and expected...make that demanded, total respect from her class. A stickler for discipline, there were certain points in the day when she'd loosen the reins and allow us to have a little fun, "visiting", as she liked to call it amongst our classmates. Every so often we'd get a little carried away, having too much fun and the noise levels would reach a fever pitch. Upon hearing and seeing us getting out of hand, Mrs. Nelson would rise to her feet and slowly place one finger up to her mouth which meant she wanted silence. Once we were all quiet, once all the noise had stopped, she would say..." Use your inside voice."

More often than not when we have a problem or find ourselves faced with a difficult set of circumstances; we'll seek direction from someone on the outside. We'll look for an answer and before we know it everyone is showing up with one, sometimes two or more. Even the person with the same problem whose answer didn't solve their problem but for some reason or another they think it will solve yours; they show up too. In time, the noise levels will rise to the point where you can't even think clearly...that's when you know the time has come...to use your inside voice.

Your inside voice, it's the one that knows you the best. Your inside voice, it's that small voice inside of you that always and without fail has your best interest at heart. Your inside voice, that's the one on the inside that only wants good things for you. Your inside voice, yeah...it's the one that speaks the softest...***but carries the most strength***.

The next time the noise levels of life become too much for you to deal with, rise to your feet, and slowly place one finger up to your mouth...and use your inside voice...

Check his feet

Shoes sir ", said Major Rawlins following the brutal beating of Private Trip in the movie, "*Glory.*" A Union patrol had apprehended Trip played by Denzel Washington and assumed him to be a deserter when in fact, he was off trying to find a pair of shoes that fit his feet. Day in and day out, the 54th Massachusetts of which he was a member endured harsh training – most in shoes too small for their feet.

"The men need shoes."

Finding a pair of shoes his size sounds simple enough but for a runaway slave turned Union soldier whose entire existence had been based on survival not convenience--not fit, access to a pair of shoes that fit was a complicated matter indeed. Upon hearing this request, Colonel Shaw assured Rawlins shoes for coloreds was on his to-do list.

"Now sir. The boy was off trying to find himself a pair of shoes."

The nature of this comment prompted the Major to visit the infirmary where the recently disciplined Private lay healing. He saw Trip's back, reduced to ribbons, the results of a severe flogging...but it was his feet that told the story. They were mangled from weeks of training in shoes that didn't fit. But mangled though they may have been, they never stopped him from training...they never stopped him from searching for shoes that fit.

"He wants to fight—same as the rest of us...more even."

Over 600,000 lives were lost during the Civil War, with heavy casualties on both sides. In retrospect, the argument can be made that no one wanted to fight more than the black man, free or slaved. While others were fighting for a way of life, he was fighting for his life.

Shoes sir...

There's a Private Trip in every city. A young black boy who set out one night in search of a pair of shoes. Shoes that will help him get to that next place in life, shoes that will tell him he can when the whole world reminds him that he can't – shoes, that fit his feet.

The men need shoes...

It sounds simple enough, but you'd be surprised how many times this simple statement falls on deaf ears. The men need shoes – the kind that'll allow them to be confident, operating in any environment. The kind that'll equip them for the unique challenges that've been set aside for them and them alone -- the kind of shoes they can walk in.

Now sir. The boy was off trying to find himself a pair of shoes.

The young black boy off trying to find himself some shoes rarely has a chance to tell this story. It might seem as though he's up to mischief, busy becoming the label society placed on him long before his arrival. Do some make poor choices, yes, but in so many other cases, the choice has already been made for him.

Close the door, he can't come in...He did it...This can't be your car...What are you doing in this neighborhood...Where'd you get that money...These words and so many others represent the flogging the black boy receives...daily.

There's a fire burning inside the young black boy. A fire to do better, to defy the odds and be everything this life says he can't be. Give him a classroom, not a jail cell. He wants a job, a business of his own one day...not a corner to hustle. A neighborhood he can come home to not one he longs to escape from...He wants to fight – same as the rest of us...more even.

The next time you see a young black boy, heading down the wrong path, don't assume he has deserted life. Instead, take a moment and look at his feet. Understand that your kind words, your voice might be the shoes that he's been off searching for. Don't wait until next time because next time might be too late – or it might never come at all...do it now, sir.

He'll light up. I've seen it. Trust me. He wants to fight – same as the rest of us...more even.

The boy just needs himself a pair of shoes...

Harriet Tubman

Harriet Tubman is without question my favorite American hero. Her story is compelling, and a study of her life will show that just like most persons of African descent living in the South during the 1800's, she was forced to live under what can only be termed as horrific conditions. Whippings, rape, starvation, and the constant duress that comes from the potential of each are only a few of the challenges that Mrs. Tubman and others like her faced daily. You probably know the story of her escaping from slavery and going on to be recognized as the most successful conductor of the Underground Railroad, but the event that led to her escape is rarely discussed.

Mrs. Tubman overheard a conversation... During this conversation, her master at the time was negotiating to sell her to a neighboring plantation roughly 8 miles down the road. While 8 miles in terms of distance is not very far...to a slave, it may as well have been a million miles away as movement between plantations by slaves was limited and, in some cases, punishable by death. Upon hearing of her imminent sale, Mrs. Tubman did one of the most powerful things a person can do with their life...she decided. She decided that she would no longer be bound. She decided that her life was her life and hers alone and that night, she escaped from slavery.

History shows that she made 19 other trips into the South to ferry family, friends, and others to freedom. Before every trip out of the South, Mrs. Tubman would gather her "passengers" and look each one in the eyes before leaving and challenge them to do the same thing she did on that faithful night...decide. Once the decision to leave was made she promised them that the destination would be sweeter than anything that they could have ever imagined.

Nothing in our lives even remotely compares to the conditions that those brave souls faced. But the one commonality in their lives and ours is that at some point...a decision must be made. Life is too short to be held by the chains of unhappiness and being content to just exist; decide to truly begin living. But here's an important point to remember. Once you execute your escape plan and begin living the life that has truly been planned for you, once you become free: be like Mrs. Tubman and go back to the other side and help ferry others to freedom. Let them know there is a destination, a place, a beautiful space designed just for them too, and to reach that place... All any of us has to do ...

Is decide.

Malcolm X

The funeral of Malcolm X was one of the largest in the history of New York City with over 30,000 mourners in attendance. In addition to this crowd there were thousands more who listened to or watched it live on radio and television. Brothers and sisters; some Muslims, some Christian, some in between gathering together to send the great shining black prince Malcolm X home. You might not have agreed with his religion, his politics, his views but no one could doubt the fire that burned within him. Malcolm X...The Protector as he had come to be known in some circles; he was ours...we were his.

The first phase of the service ended, and the time came for the pilgrimage to the cemetery where he was to be laid to rest. The procession wove its way through Harlem, the borough whose streets he once ruled, in bad ways...but later good. It wove its way through Harlem and with each step the numbers swelled as the enormity of this occasion began to resonate. Malcolm X...he was ours...we were his...

Upon arriving at the cemetery last rites were read and the command was given to bury him. He was lowered into the ground and then the most powerful scene of the day took place. The gravediggers reached for their shovels to complete the burial and it happened...Out of nowhere and in unison black men in attendance dressed in trench coats, top hats, pocket squares, in their best suits, spit-shined shoes and cuff links stopped the gravediggers. They stopped them; some Muslims, some Christians, some in between, took the shovels from them and said no..." This one is on us...Malcolm X...he was ours...we were his...we will cover this brother" ...

I used to work in sales at a cemetery. It was a sad place to be because all day, every single day death surrounded me. My duty days as they were called were draining to say the least, so I'd find myself going places to relax, calm down and decompress. Malls were my favorite places to do this and one day I stopped in one, sat down...and watched all of these alive brothers walking around...dead.

I saw young brothers with minds that have been poisoned by music and culture, alive yet dead. I saw boys, little boys, beautiful little babies tagging along, alive yet knocking on death's door. The saddest part was seeing grown brothers, alive but dead because so many times before even opening their mouths or trying their hand...they were told no.

And there stands the world, ready to grab that shovel and bury them. That has to change. You might not agree with everything he does but at the end of each day, he is yours and you are his which is why you should stop standing idly by and watching the world so quick and oh so happy to do the dirty work of burying him. Speak life into him and watch that same life be spoken into you.

Believe me when I tell you there's a **_black shining prince_** struggling to get out, a fire that burns so protect him. But until he comes out...it's your job, it's our job...

To cover that brother...

Nat Turner

Nat Turner's Slave Rebellion took place in 1831 and to this day it still stands as one of the more fascinating moments in American history. A portrait of courage, Turner spent years planning and meeting in secret with the men who would form his army and hopefully lead the charge to free his people from bondage.

Two things happened during the course of the rebellion that even Turner in all his meticulous planning couldn't have accounted for, essentially derailing their efforts. First, there was alcohol. Up until this point most of the army had only seen the fine wines, whiskies, and sipping brandy that the masters owned and indulged in from time to time. With those masters now lying dead the army had their way with these drinks and it slowed their progress considerably.

Then there was the second and most painful. Turner assumed that once he and his army rode into the slave quarters, the black community if you will, that sat on the now conquered plantations, his forces would grow. The entire plan rest on this belief that his people would join him and do something that up until that time many had never done, fight for their freedom. He was sadly mistaken.

Each time they came into a black community, Turner would look at the black men and say, ***"brother we need your help; can't get this job done without you."*** Sadly...the black men would wave them off, I'm good...that's your problem, not mine. Turner would then look at the black woman and say, "sister a hot meal, bandages for my men; will you help?" Sadly, the black women would grab her children and walk into her cabin, without so much as a crust or bread or a cool drink of water...that's your problem, not mine. Those slaves who refused to join in some sad, senseless way thought they had made it.

The rebellion failed and eventually all of the men who formed the Turner Army were caught and put to death and slavery continued for another 32 years. But one can only wonder what might have been if those same brothers and sisters who turned and walked away, saying not my problem, realized that it was...and stood up.

Their world would have been a much different place...

Our communities are still full of Nat Turner's who are striving to break free and, in the process, free those around them. It might be a relative, a friend or a child but they're fighting whatever has them bound to gain some measure of freedom. Too many times when they ride into the communities of those who think they've made it they get judged and turned away.

They see a brother, a brother who made it and ask for a hand up, not a handout...but the brother tells him "that's your problem, not mine." A sister sees another sister, doing well for herself and asks, genuinely asks if she can help her do well too but she ignores the plea, thinking about hers instead of ours; "girl that's your problem, not mine."

The truth of the matter is that it, whatever it may be, is our problem. Stop waving each other off, stop turning and walking away. Because once we embrace that truth and begin to stand up...

Our world will become a much different place...

Denmark Vesey

Did you hear the news? Lottery news I should say as last week it was revealed that a 20-year-old from Florida won the lottery estimated to have been a whopping $450 million. Let's hope he exercises wisdom because contrary to popular belief, history tells us that winning the lottery doesn't always lead to a happily ever after. No, in some cases the lives of winners are turned upside down not because of the cars, the houses or the vacations…but because of choices, more specifically, people choices.

Denmark Vesey was not your average slave. Large, powerfully built, and fluent in English, Spanish and French, he was also a skilled carpenter that made a living outside of the plantation of which he belonged. On the night of November 1, 1799 fate stepped in. While on his way home from a job he hired out on young Mr. Vesey purchased a lottery ticket. When he awoke on the morning of November 2, he found out that his life would never be the same. Denmark Vesey had won the jackpot of $1500! $1500 dollars is a good chunk of change by today's standards but back then it was a fortune. His first order of business was to purchase his freedom which he did for $600. The remaining $900 was not nearly enough to free his wife and two children but with it he was able to start his own carpentry business. His plan was to purchase their freedom with the proceeds of this venture but each time he approached their master regarding their purchase…

He was rejected…

By day he toiled away but by night, Denmark Vesey the businessman, the freed slave, the newly ordained AME minister, the lottery winner seethed with anger. Seething with anger but all the while planning. Planning to launch what would have been the largest slave rebellion the nation has ever seen. All over South Carolina, the slave community was abuzz. Known simply as The Rising, the size and scope of this operation had it succeeded would have changed the very fabric of our nation. Thousands upon thousands of slaves had pledged allegiance and stood ready to spring into action. Finally, the date was set; July 14th, 1822. But there was only one problem…someone stopped believing. Someone stopped believing and told the authorities.

Once they were alerted…Denmark Vesey, the businessman…the freed slave…the newly ordained AME minister…the lottery winner watched as his life was turned upside down. Turned upside down because ***he surrounded himself…with the wrong people.***

Some of us are not where life has called us to be because we continue to surround ourselves with the wrong people. We plan, make sacrifices, and confide. But when the time comes to go into action, things never quite come to fruition because someone on our side simply does not believe. History has shown that all it takes is one non-believer to foil the entire plan so before moving forward, check yourself. Check yourself friends and make sure you understand, believe in and you're fully committed to your mission.

But more importantly before you go into battle...check to make sure you have surrounded yourself...with the right people.

Frederick Douglass

The Autobiography of Frederick Douglass is in my opinion a must read for anyone regardless of age or race. It's an inspiring story to say the least that follows the life a great American hero. His experiences give insights into the harsh realities of slavery and the old south in ways that should make us all appreciate the struggles our ancestors had to endure. He tells the story of his mother of whom he was separated from at birth. This was the common practice on plantations so as not to allow the mother and child to form any type of a bond. Later on, Mr. Douglass relives through words the gruesome torture of his Aunt Hester, used as a bed winch by her master. But when caught spending time with a young male slave of her choice the master brutally beats her within an inch of her life.

But while there are many stories that stand out, the one that stood out the most was his visit to the home of Edward Covey. Edward Covey was what was known in those times as a "slave breaker." Yes, if you had a troublesome, rebellious Negro, slave owners throughout the South knew that Covey was the man you sent him to. Covey would work, starve, whip, and play mental games with slaves until they begged for mercy and he had plans to do the same with Mr. Douglass upon his arrival. For weeks he worked young Frederick until he dropped, fed him food unfit for animals and beat him for the smallest infraction.

This routine went on and on and just as Mr. Douglass was about to break, he made the defining choice of his life...he fought back and won. At the age of 16 he fought like his life depended on it and defeated the cruelest, most sadistic slave breaker the south had ever known and once he did, his life was forever changed. His eyes were opened; the chains fell off of his mind, his back straightened up. Most importantly, his life took on a purpose. He was no longer a slave -- on that day he became a man of purpose.

I don't know what you're going through or where you are today but there is a Covey, a slave breaker in all of our lives. It arrived with the intention of beating us down day after day keeping us from all the good that this life was meant to be. But before you give up, during those times when you feel yourself about to break remember that great American hero Frederick Douglass! Stand up to whatever it is and watch it back away. Fight like your life depends because when you do, you're sure to defeat whatever it is that has come upon you. You're sure to defeat it and when you do, watch your eyes open. When you do, notice how those chains fall off of your mind, see how your back straightens.

Most importantly...watch how much purpose this beautiful life of yours begins to hold.

I was down to Nothing

I once owned a cleaning service and let me tell you, I loved every minute of it... almost. Just like so many other small business owners, cash flow was my problem and it crippled me to the fullest. Oh, it wasn't that I didn't have clients because I had plenty; from one side of my city to the next. My problem was that my largest client where the bulk of my business was done took their time when it came time to pay the invoices. When the check came...it was great...it was the "when" that was so hard to overcome!

Through them I had 11 luxury complexes in the heart of Dallas and these properties were incredible. They were incredible, but they were killing my business. At one point, they owed me nearly $6000—a nice chunk of change for a small business or any business for that matter.

Weekdays were our workdays, and everyone knew that unless there was an emergency of some sort, weekends were off limits. Well as fate would have it, I got called down by one of the property managers for what she deemed an emergency. Seems one of my workers had gotten ahead of themselves and forgot to remove a few items from the top of the cabinets in one unit. No worries, I hurried down, finished the job, and assured her it would never happen again...But all the while I was thinking of how much easier life would be if her company would just send me my money.

A new week began and still no payment. Frustrated, I called their parent company and was assured that the check was on the way. But as the week progressed...nothing, no check, no call, nothing ... not a single cent. It got serious as payroll rolled around. We barely made payroll and with that out of the way, I needed supplies ... and food. Yes, the lags in pay had begun to impact my home and the cupboards had become extremely bare. So, I had a decision to make—food or supplies, and I chose supplies. I chose supplies because I knew without them the workers couldn't work but before I bought the supplies, I prayed that a check would be in the mailbox when I got home.

As the day progressed, my mind started to race so instead of waiting until I got to the house, I called the parent company to check the status of payment. Their accounting person told me the check was sent the previous morning which meant I would not get it for at least a couple of days. Not good because I was hungry...and didn't know how I was going to eat, but I kept working. Following that meeting with the manager I had begun to go to each apartment and check the tops of the cabinets prior to them being inspected.

Each time...it was clear of trash and debris, until this one unit. I got on my step ladder and sure enough, there was all kinds of junk up there. Tennis balls, wrappers, empty beer cans...and a large envelope. **_Curious, I opened the envelope_** and out fell a bunch of what looked like credit cards but turned out to be restaurant gift cards.

TGIFridays, Applebees, Outback, Spaghetti Warehouse; I mean these were some nice places and as hungry and worried as I was...So, I called the 800 numbers on the cards on the off chance that they still had a balance on them and to my surprise, each one of them...had a full balance. I went from being hungry to having my pick of where to eat lunch and dinner,

But it gets better...

I make it a habit of cleaning my feet on my doormat before coming into the house. Well, I got home that night and started cleaning my feet and felt something funny underneath. It was a FEDEX envelope. Turns out the parent company had sent the check the previous day...but their accounting person forgot to tell me they sent it overnight. Problems solved. In a span of roughly 4 hours, all the worries that I had concerning my situation had been taken care of.

I was down to nothing...but God was up to something.

I had a great business but barely any food at home. But when God sent me down that Saturday to clear the top of that counter...He was up to something.

For years, I've wiped my feet on doormats not just at my house but any house. All those years I thought I was just cleaning my feet, doing a common courtesy...come to find out that through that small act...God was up to something.

Supplies or food---which one would it be? I chose supplies which was an act of faith. To this day, I'm convinced that had I chose to hold off on buying supplies and instead bought groceries, I would've never been able to see what God was up to. Yes, my faith unlocked His promise and yours can too.

As we head into another day, no matter how bleak your situation may appear to be on the surface, understand that when you're down to nothing...out of groceries, no supplies, no friends, no money, this or that...keep moving especially when you're down to nothing.

Because when you're down to nothing...

God is up to something.

Cool!

This past Sunday morning I did what I've done for as many Sunday mornings as I can remember. I speed-walked, ok I ran, to the front door. I opened it and there sitting patiently at the edge of my driveway was that familiar bright blue bag containing my Sunday New York Times. Each year newspapers are folding up and closing shop, but I promise to do whatever I can to keep this one afloat as it has become a staple of my weekend.

With paper in tow, I ran back and got ready to dig into it...and this is where the problem began -- I couldn't find my glasses. I looked and looked but they were nowhere to be found. At my wits end and looking to bring a little light to the situation, I yelled, "has anyone seen my glasses?" I live alone so of course, there was no response. I chuckled and thought back to all the times growing up when my father would bellow that question out as he made plans to read his newspaper.

That's when it hit me...I think I'm becoming my father.

Cool: Somewhere along the way, a certain group of friends stopped referring to my father as Mr. Pearcey, Mr. P, or Sir...and began calling him...Cool. They never said it to his face and for me, it was never a sign of disrespect. In their minds, it was just the best word they could find to describe his demeanor. Years have gone by and those same friends still call him that same name. I asked why and one said, "Cool just acted like whatever it was...was already handled."

Some of us spend day after day, night after sleepless night, a lifetime worrying how this or that will turn out. Instead of wasting that time, instead of wasting that lifetime, call your faith into action. That doesn't mean you don't do anything, that just means you do your part. Once your part is done, walk away and rest assured...it's already handled.

It's what's in your head: My junior year in high school, I finally got my hair faded. It was a slight fade, but even that was a major departure from what I'd worn up until then. Now, everyone knows where there's a fade, a brush and stocking cap can't be far behind and I was no different.

First time my old man came in my room and saw me brushing my hair, prepping to put that stocking cap on, he chuckled, and told me "cats" in his day did the same thing. He laughed some more and just as he was turning to leave, he paused, looked at me said, "You can do whatever you want to the outside of your head, but remember; it's what's inside in your head that counts." There's nothing like the satisfaction that comes from getting a great haircut. Who doesn't like that? Great haircuts are just that, great, but it's important to understand that underneath that great haircut...the inside, is where the power to shape and change your life is found.

Run: When my father first began running, he got a lot of strange looks. People laughed and thought he was crazy. Neighbors asked him what he thought he was doing and wondered aloud how long "that" would last. Friends would snicker, tease and poke fun at school. As time went on, a funny thing happened, those same people who laughed, wondered, snickered, so on and so forth...became his biggest supporters. He told me all the time there were a lot of mornings he didn't want to run...but he ran anyway, because he knew somebody needed a push, somebody needed inspiration and that's what they got when they saw him out there.

I used to run exclusively at night because I didn't want anyone to see me. One morning I woke up and decided the day was too beautiful to wait, so I laced up my shoes and ran. In the beginning, I got my fair share of strange looks. Over the years, the ones behind those strange looks became the first ones to shout out a word of encouragement. They'll blow a horn or stop me in the store and ask for a tip. Some days, I really don't want to run. Just like my father I do it anyway...because somebody needs a push, somebody needs inspiration and that's what they get when they see me out there. Today, go for a run...at the office, at home, with your wife or husband. Go for a run and keep running because you never know who needs to see you out there.

Here's the funny part about him losing his glasses...9 times out of 10, they were sitting right there on top of his head. Here's the even funnier part, when I went running through my house searching for mine, I looked in the mirror...and mine were sitting right there...on top of my head.

I think I'm becoming my father. Things don't bother me like they used to. I do my part, rest on my faith, and let it go. It seems to always work out. I get great haircuts, but understand that what's inside – my thoughts, are what's most important. I run, even on the days I don't want to because somebody is watching, and they need me to run more than I do. I think I'm becoming my father and you know what...

It's actually kinda of Cool...

We Almost Never met

For nearly 30 years my father proudly served in the US Army and as a result he is full of stories about places he has gone; people he has seen and of course, wars he has fought in. I recall one night he and I were sitting on the back porch after my first year away from college, shooting the breeze, having father and son time and the subject of his military service came up. Out of the blue he said, ***"You know you and I almost never met."*** Confused I shot back at him, "What do you mean?"

On a warm night in Vietnam after another long day, my father leaned up against a jeep and watched the sun go down. A world away, his bride was pregnant with me and his thoughts were on family, but some of the guys in his company were calling him to join the party. Each time they called he waved them off saying thanks, but no thanks. They kept after him, he kept saying no until he finally gave in, came in, and took a seat. He estimates not 30 seconds after he had sat down that jeep, the one he was leaning up against was hit by an enemy rocket and exploded. "Had I not moved we would never have met."

While I enjoy hearing the stories of war my father, our soldier tells from time to time, I'm most touched by the war I saw him wage firsthand. I'm touched by the way he stood and fought to raise his six children during a day and age when most men would've taken off and run. He wasn't perfect but then, who is...but he stayed and that part of him was perfection. Every time I eat a pancake. I remember how he would wake up at 3 in the morning; fix a batch for his kids and leave them warming in the oven before heading out the door for formation.

I chuckle when I hang up a shirt or pair of pants, remembering an encounter I had with my alarm company. My system needed repair and my alarm box is located in my closet. When the technician arrived. I led him to my room and into the closet so he could take care of the situation. He surveyed the surrounding and then looked over at me and asked if I was raised military. I told him I was. He replied, "I figured so." I asked how. He said, "Only a man raised military would have his bed made up, his closet straight and his bathroom clean like this."

I got stopped in a hallway at a place I used to work by a person I had never spoken to. She asked if I were military. I told her I was raised military but how did she know? She said," Your shoes; only a military man would have a high gloss shine like that on them." There are mornings or nights when I don't want to go out and run but then I stop and remember that until recently my father, was out there in his nineties...it makes my decision to go a whole lot easier.

If you're blessed to still have your father, go see him, call him, write him this week...let him know how glad you are the two of you met. If he's gone on, live, work, and play this week in his honor.

I guarantee you...your life wouldn't have been the same without him...

Flow Free

I don't know about you, but I hardly ever see anyone out in the driveway washing the car anymore. In fact, as I sit back, I can only think of a couple of people on my street who still do it this way, including myself as I roll my car out of the garage every so often to clean it up. Hey, I guess we can thank all the quick service, drive-thru car washes that are on just about every corner these days...that and, as my father says, the fact that the world has gone out and got in such a big hurry! A few weeks back, I took the time to pull out the bucket and towels and hand wash my car. As I went through the process, I remembered how much fun we would have as children whenever a neighbor would pull the car out of the garage, park it in the driveway and give it a good old-fashioned washing. Now, we wouldn't help. No; that's not where our fun was had.

My little crew and I were far too cool for that. Instead, we would stand by and wait for whoever it was to begin rinsing their car off...and that's when it all began. As the water from the rinsing started running down the street on cue, we'd grab a blade of grass, a small stick or something light, throw it in the water and watch it flow! Every so often something would clog up or block the path and one of us would reach down and open it up. Might be a can, might be a rock, might be an old newspaper but whatever it was one of us would bend down, move it out of the way and before we knew it...things would start to flow again...

You know every so often we come out of a situation in our life journey that causes us to become dirty, just like a car on its daily travels...and we find ourselves in need of a good old-fashioned washing. It could be a failed relationship or a job loss or a myriad of other personal or professional hurts. We pull out, wash off the hurt, the pain, the blood, sweat and tears...and watch as they go rolling down the street.

But in some cases, we don't come out all the way clean because we forget to wash off that one important stain that stain of unforgiving on our hearts. While all those other forms of debris that have gathered and are now being washed off are rolling down the streets the stain of unforgiving on our hearts continues to block our path. Friend at some point and at some point, soon open your garage and pull yourself out into your personal driveway and give yourself a good old-fashioned washing. For some of us, most of us, a quick service, drive-thru won't do. We need a good one. A good one unlike any we've ever had before and this time...let's be sure to wash that stain of unforgiving off...because behind this stain is where our blessings can be found.

And when we wash off this stain, despite all the hurt and pain we may have endured and what it has come to symbolize...

Things will start to flow again…

Raymon

Without question the most fun part of Christmas as a child was what became known around our house as...wakeup time. Wakeup time meant my mother coming in and rousing us from our sleep. All it took that day was the slightest touch because like most children we slept with one eye open that night. Once we felt her touch we'd hop out of bed and take off running down the hallway like a thundering herd! The time had come; we were finally getting the chance to open up all those beautifully wrapped gifts!

One particular Christmas, wakeup time for some reason just wouldn't come. Worried, I remember us going into our parent's room, asking my mother if it were time yet. She led us down the hallway and into the den to check the clock and the clock said no so she sent all of us back to bed. All of us with the exception of my oldest brother who was home from college and chose to stay up that night reading and studying. More time passed and each visit we made to their room she'd patiently walk us down the hall to check the clock. But each time the clock said no.

On our final visit to our parent's room I remember my mother meeting us at her door. By this time, she'd become somewhat confused herself. She led us down the hallway to the den one last time. Only this time instead of just looking at the clock...she turned on the television. Back in those days you only had a handful of channels but there was that one channel that always showed the time. She put the television on that channel and as it turned out...there was about a two-hour difference between the time our clock said and the actual time. Just then my oldest brother burst into laughter. Come to find out...this dude had been turning the clock back all night so he could get a little more time to study.

It stands as one of my most fond and funniest Christmas memories. And although it happened so many years ago, I still consider it one of the most precious gifts I ever received.

Presents get old; you outgrow them, you don't use them, you exchange them, you spend too much...so on and so forth. But the presence of the ones you love, the special people and the memories you make together they never get old, you never outgrow them, they're always useful.

Most of all...they're priceless!

Pastor … will you pray for me?

No matter the day or time, I always start my run in my neighborhood. I've become such a fixture on these streets that the dogs don't even bark at me anymore; they just stand, stare, and give that little doggy yell of approval. When it comes to the neighbors, they send out all kinds of acknowledgments.

There's the guy who owns the glass shop on the end of my street who always asks me how many I plan to do. I'm not sure is usually my response but I always promise to run one for him. We have the brother a few doors down who coaches kids who asks that I do a few strides for his team…" of course" is always my response. "Back at it I see", is how my Muslim neighbor greets me…I respond with a shrug of the shoulders, a smile, and a quick exchange of pleasantries.

While I appreciate all of the kind words, the most unique comments come from these two older African women who live on opposite ends of the community. Both still have their thick accents which tell me they came to America later in life but no worries as they speak clearly. As I pass the home of the first one, she will smile and say, "Hello Pastor, how are you on this day?" "Fine thank you" smiling but never breaking stride but always thinking one day I will have to stop and tell her…***I'm not a Pastor.***

In another, oh I'd say three-fourths of a mile, I come to the next African women I spoke of…and she gives a similar greeting. "Hello Pastor, I wish many blessings to you, sir." "Thank you, same to you", is how I respond with a nod and a smile while keeping my pace and thinking…I don't preach woman… As I exit the subdivision, I always find myself wondering how I'm going to break the news to them…

🌲 🌲 🌲

The corral at a distance event is where runners huddle in mass and await the start of their race. This is a place reserved only for runners and once you enter, there is no exit. At that point, it's just you alone with your thoughts about the road and the race ahead.

You see all kinds of looks in the corral. Some looks say, "What have I gotten myself into" …I've worn that one a time or two. Others will say things like, "Did I train enough", "Am I really ready for this", "Will what I ate this morning be enough", "Have I got what it takes" …You see all of those and then some.

This past December I ran the Dallas Half Marathon and let me tell you it was brutal with hills, inclines, dips, twist and turns of all kinds. And just like all those times before, we gathered in the corral…that lonely place reserved only for runners with all of the aforementioned looks…and then some…

I was in my zone, with my playlist queued up and a laser focus when out of nowhere, another runner tapped me on the shoulder. I removed my headphones and before I could ask what he needed he said, "Pastor...will you pray for me" ...

I thought about those two African women and my first impulse was to tell him I'm not a Pastor and move on but instead, we bowed, and I prayed for him. It wasn't a long prayer, but it was a strong prayer and when it was over, we embraced briefly and gave each other one last look of encouragement. The most interesting part of that entire exchange is that after praying for him...I felt stronger, more determined...emboldened...confident.

As I ran those 13.1 miles I kept coming back to that prayer, to that runner who I had never seen before or since. What I realized is that God sent him to me for prayer not because he needed one but because I did. I'm just glad that I didn't turn him away because without that prayer, without him calling me Pastor, I would have surely missed the blessing of finishing the race.

God might not send it to you in the most conventional way, but he knows what you need. Your responsibility is to be open and willing to receive it as your willingness to do so will open the door to the blessing that will allow you to finish the race...whatever and wherever it might be...

The Final Lesson

If you live long enough and your parents do too, the dynamics of your family are sure to evolve. Parents who were once providers, become dependent on children as age, nature, and time become factors. My siblings and I find ourselves at this stage with our father as he continues to battle a series of health challenges.

Seeing him in the requisite hospital garb of gown, tubes, bags, with a monitor beeping in the background just loud enough to keep you apprised is indeed a sight. It's a sight because when I look at him in that bed, I flash to memories of the man who has always been in tip top shape. I go back to the man who ran 2-3 miles a day, sometimes twice a day – at 80! I thought about those times and looked at his once strong now withering body connected to devices going every which way and jokingly thought to myself ...

"I don't know this guy..."

I went out to the hallway, found a bench, and untied my left shoe. I'm a runner just like my father, and my left arch, has been giving me troubles of late. So, every so often, I'll untie that shoe and sometimes, go so far as to take the shoe all the way off. Sitting there, I thought back to him telling me years ago to make sure I put supports in my shoes to protect my arches. I didn't listen then and I'm paying for it now, but as soon as I arrived at home, I went out and got myself a pair of arch supports.

I didn't drive home last week, instead I rode with my sister. My car was making a funny sound and with so much at stake, I didn't want to risk getting stuck somewhere on the side of the road. I got back to town and took it over to my mechanic for a look see. He hooked it up to the machine and said everything checked out. Then he turned and said, "you got hold to some bad gas man."

My father swears by Shell gas, that good gas as he likes to call it. For as long as I've been driving, he's advised me to only fill up with Shell. I follow this advice as much as possible, but with my schedule being what it has been here of late, all I need to see is the letters G A S when I'm on E, and I'm stopping. When my tank got back down to E this last time, I pulled over at a Shell station and filled it up with that good gas ... car runs just like new.

Everyone in my office, the entire team has been sick at some point during these last few months. Colds, the flu, strep throat ... if you can name it chances are, someone on my team has been forced to endure it ... everyone except me that is. I attribute this to a lot of things most important of all, my diet. For years, vegetables have been the foundation of my father's lifestyle. I can remember sitting down to the dinner table and seeing his plate filled with vegetables from one side to the next ... and I hated it.

During the winter months, he'd look across the table and say, "I could walk downtown right now with no jacket or shirt on. I'd get cold … but I wouldn't get sick, because all the good things I eat would protect me." Even though I work in an office where everyone is sniffling, sneezing, and coughing, I haven't gotten sick. I'm still standing not because I pop pills or anything of the sort. No, I'm still going strong because when I sit down to dinner, my plate looks a lot like my fathers used to, filled with vegetables from one side to the next … and I love it.

These precious lessons and a few others came to mind as I sat there that day. Then it hit me, the way he's lying in that bed … that too is a lesson. You see, two weeks ago, the doctors told us his transition was underway and by weeks end, it would be complete … but he's still here … he's still fighting. He's still fighting, and I'm convinced that this is the final lesson he wants to impart on his friends and family. A lesson that says no matter what the odds may say, or how they're stacked against you, show up … and fight.

***

The time came for us to leave and we began making our way out of the room. I told him I'd be back in a day or so, but doubted he heard me as he'd been incoherent for several days. Before leaving, ***I softly rubbed the top of his head***, something that has become our signature goodbye. Out of nowhere and to my surprise, he cracked the biggest smile … I smiled back and thought to myself …

Yeah … I know this guy …

Sometimes, that pain be necessary

The Grammy's are widely recognized as the biggest night of the year for the music industry. Artists, musicians, and producers line up, dress up and pray that they get called up in recognition of their creative endeavors. I watched a little of it this year but not much. Jazz is my favorite music and it barely gets a mention on the show, but I tuned in just long enough to see who would win Song of the Year. No surprise there as anywhere you go you hear Bruno so it stands to reason he would walk away with it and he did. Good for him and that's quite an honor. But if it's an honor to be recognized for having the Song of the Year, imagine what it must feel like to be recognized for having...the Song of the Century.

With the abolishment of slavery, ***Southerners saw their control of black lives change overnight***, literally. Since they could no longer control blacks through ownership, a new form emerged, lynching. Lynching was quite simply a spontaneous act of "justice" meted out against blacks for the slightest transgression. It was simple. All that was needed was a rope, an angry mob, a black (usually a black male), a tree and a reason. They happened all throughout the South and the most horrifying part of it all is that when the lynching was done, when he, she or they were pronounced dead, they were not taken down. No, the indignity continued as they were left hanging from trees for days at a time as a constant reminder for all to see.

A poem entitled, "Strange Fruit" was written about the phenomenon of Southern lynching's. This poem was later put to music by the great jazz singer Billie Holiday and in 1999, "Strange Fruit" was recognized as by Time Magazine as the Song of the Century. Singing it in the South was a dangerous proposition as protesting crowds surrounded venues where Billie played daring her to perform it. Club owners in New York where Billie Holiday made her name would only allow her to sing it every so often. For days after her performance attendance would be down as the pain of the song hung heavy in and seemingly haunted the venue. But when she was allowed to perform this song, it was a sight to behold. The room stilled itself, the audience fell into a trance and a single light fell on Billie...

Southern trees bear a strange fruit
Blood on the leaves and blood on the root
Black bodies swinging in the Southern breeze
Strange fruit hanging from the poplar trees

Pastoral scene of the gallant South
The bulging eyes and the twisted mouth
Scent of magnolias sweet and fresh
Then the sudden smell of burning flesh

Here is the fruit for the crows to pluck
For rain to gather, for wind to suck
For the sun to rot, for the tree to drop
Here is a strange and bitter crop

She didn't just sing the song. For that brief point in time she became it and when she was done, she had nothing left to give. It had taken everything out of her. Everyone noticed the pain it caused her. From peers to fans to critics and beyond, everyone noticed. Down Beat Magazine, the world's premier jazz publication of that period asked her why she continued to perform a number that caused her so much pain. She responded by saying, "Sometimes that pain be necessary ..."

Some of the best things in life, some of the lessons that hold the most value are the ones that are most filled with hurt. A shattered dream or hope but tomorrow brings another day. In the perfect world that none of us live in we wish, hope and dream that the hurt never comes our way. But in the imperfect world that we all live in, hurt is a part of it. There's no getting around it and nothing left to do other than realize that in order to get to that better place, learn that lesson and live your best life...

Sometimes...that pain be necessary...

The Leftovers

Man, I love the holidays. I love the beauty of the malls with trees, lights, smiles, and ornaments adorning them. I love riding through neighborhoods and seeing well-lit houses with drapes pulled just enough to allow a peek at the Thanksgiving and Christmas décor inside. I love the way the weather gets colder around the holidays and even the coldest hearts get warmer. I love Charlie Brown specials...yes, there...I said it. But most of all...I love the food, especially the leftovers. Yes, I love the leftovers. In my opinion, they're the best part of the holiday and the meal.

Prior to my newfound love for cooking, leftovers –not gifts, were the thing I used to look forward to them the most around this time of the year. Meats seemed to taste better the second time around when seasonings have seeped in. The same can be said for vegetables. Desserts and breads are far moister the next day and literally melt in your mouth. I cherished every gift I get but trust me when I tell you there have been years, several years when I have gone home to visit family and friends for the holidays and ran off and forgot my gifts. But one thing I can say for certain is that I have never forgotten the leftovers.

Those are the best gifts.

Even though it's November, Christmas is fast approaching which means a New Year can't be far behind. During this year some of us have had some incredible holidays with even more incredible meals. Not the traditional ones but ones that have been divinely set aside for us and us alone.

We've had holidays called college graduation followed by nice meals. We've had holidays called relationship restoration and they too were followed beautiful meals. Some of us have had holidays called new business ownership, overcoming health challenges and addictions and all of those were followed by a deeply fulfilling meal. Each of those meals no matter what occasion precipitated them or when they were consumed have one thing in common; that's right...they've got leftovers.

No matter how large or small they may have been, there were some leftovers. Leftovers are those valuable lessons that you learned along the way to your holiday and while you consumed the meal that followed. Friend, there may come a time when no matter how much you cherish the gift you receive on your holiday; you leave it behind—you forget it. But do yourself a favor. Learn to love, never leave, and never forget the leftovers--those special, beautiful, and incredible life lessons you learned along the way.

Those...are the best gifts...

Drapetomania

Breeding among slaves was highly encouraged and expected on plantations. In the eyes of the slave masters more slaves made meant more work done which ultimately meant more profits being generated. The sanctity of marriage was never recognized as the chief concern for the master was breeding no matter how it came to pass. A married female slave with a single male slave or vice versa; it made the slave owner no difference as all he wanted was another slave body, another free laborer. But while masters focused on breeding life and made sure their slaves did the same, diseases were also being bred.

The unsanitary conditions led to all types. From cholera to hepatitis, from tuberculosis to typhoid, influenza and beyond, slave quarters were the perfect breeding ground for diseases. And while all of the aforementioned caused slave owners throughout the south many a sleepless night a new one was uncovered in 1851; Drapetomania. Drapetomania was described as a mental disease that caused slaves to harbor thoughts of freedom to the point where they would actually attempt to escape.

All slaves were susceptible to this disease but upon a closer examination, southern "doctors" made a startling discovery. They found that while any slave could be stricken with drapetomania the vast majority of the ones that came down with it...were ***young black men between the ages of 16 to 25.*** Young black men who had the audacity to believe that they had a future that extended beyond the bonds of slavery were teeming with this illness.

Medical science tried but alas no pill, no capsule, no tablet, gel, or ointment was found to be a suitable cure. And since no medical cure could be found slave owners resorted to doing what they knew best; they beat them. Any slave especially a young black male slave as they had the audacity to believe they had a future, that showed traces of drapetomania was severely punished.

The young black male slave was punished to the point that he stopped believing. Yes, he stopped believing because contrary to popular belief, slaves were not born...they were made and when they were born, they were born believing hence the yearning to be free. He was punished to the point where he gave up hope...he was punished to the point where he gave up on thinking that he had a future.

So, he stayed bound...

Drapetomania was never recognized by mainstream medicine and was eventually dismissed as nothing more than a southern medical myth but the remnants remain. All over American young black men are being beat down, literally, and figuratively; punished to the point where in some instances they've all but given up. But those chains that have them bound can be broken, all it takes is a little love.

If you see a young black man with head held low...tell him he was built to believe...

If he looks back at you with doubt in his eyes remind him that he was conceived through hope...

And above all when he looks as though he is about to give up...remind that young brother that the future, contrary to what he's been led to believe ... belongs to him...

Easy Wasn't Always Easy

Statistics is one of the most challenging courses any college student will ever enroll in. To this day I do not understand why any student on any campus is forced to endure that torture. And to this day I promise you I have not used any of the material I learned in that classroom...

But I did learn a valuable life lesson...

The man who taught my Statistics class went by the name of Mr. Penney. I can still remember sitting in his classroom and watching him effortlessly working through those problems on the blackboard like it was nothing...it was equal parts amazing and frustrating. It was amazing because of his strong command of the subject matter. It was so strong that he actually wrote the textbook we used in class. It was frustrating because I, like so many other students in the class was struggling, saw no value in the material -- but I also knew that in order to graduate I had to take and pass it.

The session before the first test came and the classroom was full, with hands being raised all over the place asking this question and that one. It was intense as for many of us, years of hard work on campus, graduation invitations, job offers and freedom from the drudgery of being a student hung in the balance. He answered a lot of questions that night and although I doubt that I've used any of the material from that course I've hung onto this his one piece of advice for years.

Before leaving he calmed the room and took control in a different way. He looked out and softly said, "The test is going to be a challenge, but you can do it. Here's the key: find the easy problems and finish them. Finish the easy problems because this will give you the confidence and momentum that you need to take on the hard ones. And when you feel like you can't finish the hard ones think about how you overcame those easy ones...*because they weren't always easy*" ...

This life is nothing more than one big test filled with hard problems and easy ones. The mistake so many of us make when we face one of those hard problems is thinking we can't overcome it. Finances, relationships, parenting you name it; those hard problems stop us in our tracks.

If we just took a moment to stop and think about those easy problems and how we overcame them, this test becomes so much easier. Moving forward friend when you're faced with a hard problem think about how well you did on those easy ones because the truth to the matter is...

They weren't always easy...

Key Words

The Internet...some have called it the most powerful communications tool ever created. Want to know how much money you have...just log into your account...online. Your bank account and all the debits and credits will *magically*...appear! There's social media driven by the Internet. Social media has allowed us to connect with new friends and build amazing new relationships that we might not ever have been able to do. It's also given us the ability to reconnect with old friends, pick up where we left off and as a result, life becomes that much sweeter. All...driven by the Internet. Too hurried to watch the morning or evening news, no worries...no worries at all. Just tap into the Internet and you'll get articles, stories, and front pages from all over the world sent to you hot off the presses. It's amazing...

But here's the thing. The entire Internet is driven...by key words. Yes, it's true. You can find whatever you want to find on the Internet...as long as you're using the right key words.

Say you want a bright red 1986 Corvette with 130,000 miles in Omaha, Nebraska...type those key words into the search engine and watch that vehicle appear. An old friend you reconnected with thanks to the Internet is getting married and you haven't a thing to wear. Type in clothing stores, your size, the color of your shoes...the whole nine...and everything you need will be right there at your disposal.

Yes, ***you can find anything you want*** on the Internet...as long as you're using...the right key words.

🌲 🌲 🌲

The Internet is an amazing tool that can double as a metaphor for life. Think about it for a minute if you will. You can find anything you want on the Internet...as long as you're using the right key words, but you can also find anything in life...

As long as you're using the right key words.

Thinking about opening that business one day...don't say "I might" ...say "I will" ...then go and register the name and watch how quickly things move from there. Speak it into existence...

Single mother in school working hard to get through but you keep hearing the words, "I can't"...start saying, "I can"...then go out and buy a frame for your diploma and a nice dress to wear on graduation night no matter how far away it might be....I guarantee, you'll be there...Your words are your power...

Looking for a new job—that new job is also looking for you. It's just waiting for you to say the right things, key words that let it know the time has come to make an introduction. Change your words...you can change your life....

No matter what it is or how impossible it may seem, remember, you can find whatever you want in life...as long as you're using...

The right key words...

Your Heat Sheet

This past weekend I competed in and finished another race, the Dallas Marathon. Unlike last year when I ran the full 26.2 miles, this year, I competed in a five-person relay and I'm equally proud of that accomplishment.

The course was still a monster, with cold, whistling winds dropping the temperature into the 30's at race time. The fact that I've been sick for the past couple of weeks made it even more difficult. But I made it, with a little help from my friends.

I tell people all the time that the race is the culmination of a celebration and an experience like no other. Leading up to the race, you have access to a ton of cool stuff including shirts, hoodies, caps, energy bars -- some really, interesting energy bars, drinks...and an assortment of other trinkets.

It gets better after the race....

After the race of course, you get your medal...and that's when the party really begins. There's fruit, ice cream, pizza and a nice spread the race organizers put on that includes – free beer – too bad I'm not a drinker! These things are given out at the conclusion of every race. But there is one all-important piece that runners get upon crossing the finish line during the winter races. It's more important than hot chocolate, cold beer, bagels, fruit, or any shake you can find. That piece is called — the heat sheet.

Here's the thing. No matter how cold or windy it may be...you're going to sweat, your body warms up tremendously and you're going to sweat. But when you cross the finish line...you begin to cool off, but you're still wet from sweating which can lead to hypothermia.

Many a runner has made the mistake of not grabbing and wrapping their bodies in a heat sheet and paid dearly in the days that follow. Colds, the flu, sinus infections, even pneumonia can set in during that time of excitement when the race was completed as runners lose sight of the fact that there are others to be run.

For these reasons and many more, seasoned runners will take the water, the fruit, the carbs, and the beer when they finish a race, but the first thing they seek...is the heat sheet...

It protects them...
It prepares them for the next race...
It says, "I won't let you waste the hard work you've put in" ...
But above all...

The heat sheet...it's the thing keeps them warm.

Some of you are in the winters of our life, running this race or the next one. You cross the finish line with arms held high, to cheers, beers, medals, and all. You're wet with sweat from the just completed race. You reflect while you're wet, you smile while you're wet, laugh heartily and think grand thoughts. Then the next race comes, and you can't seem to make it...you fall down, stagger, give up...lose.

The reason this happens is because you didn't grab your heat sheet. Friend, as you continue to make your way through the winters of life, and you finish one race after another...don't forget to grab your heat sheet...

It protects you from all the outside forces...
It prepares you for whatever the next race in the winter of life may be...
It says, "I won't let you waste all the hard work you've put in...personally or professionally to get to this point...but, most of all...

It's the thing that keeps you warm...

Water It

One of the things that most attracted me to the home I just purchased was the yards. **The front yard has a porch**—something I've longed for since moving from my childhood home. When I was growing up, I spent countless hours sitting on that old front porch and I always told myself that one day, I'd have one of my own. Now I do.

The backyard is cool too with a nice patio area and an incredible view. But what really sold me on the backyard was the landscaping which includes two rows of rose bushes surrounding the perimeter of the yard. I loved how those rose bushes sat—they took me back. When my mother was alive, she had some in our front yard and I remember how big, bold, and beautiful they were and how they breathed so much life into our lives. I wanted that for this new space.

I first saw the house in January but by the time I settled on it was Spring—and those rose bushes were in full bloom. Well, a funny thing happened between the time I made my offer and closed on the house...the owner stopped watering the yards. In this Texas heat, especially on this current stretch of 100-degree temperatures, not a good idea.

The owner stopped watering the yards and whereas the yards were once lush and green...they now stood as dry and yellow. The trees that rose up to greet me that first time I came over were begging for water; so too were the hedges. And those rose bushes...not a bloom in sight.

No worries I thought, I've got just the solution, my yard guy. I called him, told him I had a new address and needed him to come by and, "do his thing." I wasn't home when he arrived, but I sent him a text to cut the grass, edge of course, trim the hedges and pull up those dead rose bushes in the back.

Upon my return I noticed that he had done an incredible job of mowing, edging and trimming--- but he forgot to pull up those dead rose bushes. Confused I called and asked why—why didn't he finish that part of the task that I was paying for?

"I didn't see any dead rose bushes back there man" he said ...to which I responded, "The only rose bushes back there are the dead ones" ...And this is where the conversation became interesting. He explained to me that the most resilient and strongest plants in the world...are flowers. They look brown and dead on the outside he said but, on the inside, they're still very much alive...He ended the conversation with a hearty laugh saying, "I didn't see no dead rose bushes Lynn...I just saw flowers that need some watering" ...

Over the course of the next week, I made it my business to water the yards, but I gave those rose bushes extra attention. Early in the morning and late at night while I unpacked and staged the house, that water was going. The first few days I saw nothing...and then one morning as I was leaving I came out to turn the water off—and what do you know...I saw a flash of color...those rose bushes that I was ready to pull up and leave for dead, had once again begun to bloom. My yard guy was right...

All they needed was some watering.

If you look in the mirror, you might see a dry plant with thorns, withered from that stretch of life that we all go through at some point where nothing seems to be going our way. Keep looking. Some, yourself included, have left that plant you see for dead—ready to pull it up and discard it. On the outside, things look bad but, on the inside, you're still very much alive...all you need is some water.

So, this week, water yourself with...

I can.
I will.
I'm stronger than this.
I'm confident.
I'm a finisher.
I'll find a way.
I'm a winner...and I refuse to settle.

Start doing that daily, morning, noon, night, and all throughout the day. Then step back in front of that mirror. You'll notice flashes of color. You'll see flashes of color and more with each passing day. From this point forward whenever you see a broken, dry, withered and worn bush staring at you...understand that there's a beautiful flower, full of life...waiting to bloom.

All it needs...is some watering...

The Scottsboro Boys

In March of 1931 on a train travelling through Tennessee, nine teenage black boys got an up close and personal look at the monster that is racism. Living in the deep South as they had all of their lives, I'm sure they had seen it before but nothing like what they were about to experience. These boys were just that, boys. This is important to note **because in the Jim Crow South every black male was referred to as a boy,** no matter their age. But these boys, whose ages ranged from 13 to 18 were just that, boys.

Hitching a ride on a train without authorization or being a "Ho Bo" as it came to be known was a crime. The train that these young boys, these Ho Bo's were travelling on was eventually stopped by the local authorities as Hoboing had become all too prevalent and, in some cases, dangerous.

Everyone was seized and searched both white and black. In an effort to save themselves from the law, several of the young White Ho Bo's concocted a plan. They accused these nine black boys of attacking and beating them. Two young White girls got in on the act and accused them of rape and set the stage for what became one of the grossest miscarriages of justice in American history.

The case was taken to Scottsboro, Alabama and these nine young black boys became known as The Scottsboro Boys. They languished on the Alabama death row awaking each day knowing that it could be their last based on accusations that had no merit whatsoever. The case went on even as one of the young white women came forward and told the courts that it was all one big lie...but the state continued to try them.

The public marched. All throughout America, the public marched. As far away as Berlin, Germany, and Moscow of the old Soviet Union, the public marched in honor of The Scottsboro Boys. But when the marches ended, everyone went home while those eight young black boys, now eight because the ninth, a 13-year-old was deemed too young to stand trial and was allowed to go free, sat on death row...for two decades...20 years...

What sticks out to me most is that these nine youngsters who, in my mind, can only be described as heroes were travelling alone. Travelling alone in a place and landing in a situation they were ill-equipped to handle. I've often wondered how different their fates could have been if a man had been travelling along to guide them. A man capable and kind enough to tell them this way, not that way; a man willing to say my way, not your way son...because your way might sound good to you, but I've tried it and, son, I know where it leads.

There may never be another case like The Scottsboro Boys, but our communities are still filled with young boys travelling in places with the potential of landing in situations that they are ill-equipped to handle. Do us all a favor...if you see one travelling alone on his way to a situation, go out of your way to help him find his way.

His life can be so much different, with a capable, kind, willing man there to guide him...

A Period and A Comma

I can probably type between 85 and 100 words per minute, maybe more depending on the combination of words you throw at me. I guess that's about average speed but average or not, that's the speed that gets the job done but trust me when I tell you it wasn't always that easy. I remember enrolling in a typing class during my sophomore year of high school. It was so awkward trying to find the correct placements for this finger and that finger but over the course of time we got the hang of it. By year's end my skills could be labeled as decent...just above hunt and peck status.

I've gotten better over time, but you know in all my years of typing there's still one area that gives me trouble. Always and without fail, day in and day out I find myself having trouble distinguishing between the period key and the comma key. I'll be typing along, hitting this key and that one then out of nowhere it'll happen; I'll hit the period key and instead hit the comma key and vice versa. No worries though as I simply backspace and correct the mistake. I'm happy to report that after all these years I am getting better, but it still stands as one of my greatest typing challenges.

A period and a comma are two little punctuation marks. ***There isn't a whole lot of difference in how they*** look but there is a world of difference in what they mean. A comma means to pause while a period...a period means it's over. A comma is used to give space while a period...a period says there is no more space to give because the end has come. A comma says there's more to come while a period...a period says there's nothing left...And while there are only subtle differences in the way they look, where they're placed can change everything.

A period and a comma are two little punctuation marks. Not a whole lot of difference in the way they look but as I said before, there's a world of difference in what they mean. What I've learned is that periods and commas have a place in reading and writing but they also have a place in life. How many times in life have you used a period when God was trying to use a comma?

You were denied a promotion on the job and instead of continuing to bring your best day in and day out, you used a period and started being average...when God intended to use a comma because there was so much more job to come. You use a period in a relationship after a heated conversation...when God knew that he or she was the one...and He intended to place a comma there just so the two of you could...pause. You use a period on a child because you feel like you have nothing left when God intended for you to use a comma because He sees so much more...

Be careful of how you choose to punctuate your life. Get to know when life is calling for you to use a period and when it is telling you to use a comma.

Because while there are only subtle differences in the way they look, where they are placed in your life...

Can change everything....

A Lesson Before Dying

A Lesson Before Dying...now that my friend is a good book. In fact, it is one of my favorite books. I loved it when I was younger...I love it more now that I'm older. It's a poignant tale set just after the Great Depression in the poor Bayou region that revolves around Jefferson; a young black boy who finds himself in the wrong place at the wrong time during a period when it could be argued that there was no right place or time for his kind. To be more specific, Jefferson and two friends entered a white-owned liquor store; an argument ensued with said owner and it quickly escalated into a gunfight. When it was over...3 people were dead...the only one standing was Jefferson.

Although he had no gun, fired no shots and his innocence was obvious, Jefferson was charged with the crime. His attorney put up a "fight" saying that his client was no smarter than a hog and incapable of a crime of this sort. The jury concurred...but Jefferson was still sentenced to death. He accepted his death sentence but sadder yet was the fact that Jefferson accepted being compared to a hog. He started acting like one, thinking like one and in the process drifted into a dark, lonely place.

His godmother, resigned to the fact that her godson would soon be executed, wanted to make sure Jefferson left this life proper, not as a hog. But in order to do so he had to be taught something that she couldn't teach. She couldn't teach it because she had never lived it, so she enlisted the help of Grant Wiggins the young black schoolteacher to teach Jefferson one last lesson before dying: that lesson...how to be a man...

All over America today, stories like this one play out; some literally, some figuratively because too many young black boys are lost and just like Jefferson, they believe themselves to be no better than a hog. They worship rappers and music challenging them to be, "about that life" ...only to find out that they only have one life to live and the life those rappers speak of, the one those black boys so blindly follow...isn't really "about" anything.

They desecrate their bodies with piercings and tattoos...and when they show up for the interview...no one will hire them. No one will hire them and since they chose to be "about that life" education was never a priority so as a result they find themselves in the wrong place at the wrong time. But if they had a man, if they had a Grant Wiggins, maybe just maybe, those wrong places and times would somehow, some kind of way become right...

The next time you see "Jefferson" don't just shake your head when you see him sagging...remind him that he's better than that. Don't act deaf when you hear vile words spewing from "Jefferson's" mouth...instead, encourage him with yours. Somehow, some kind of way: get through...to...him...She, though she is strong and brave, can't teach it because she hasn't lived it but it's long overdue.

It's long overdue and sadly, ***so many of them will continue dying until more of us become willing to teach them the lesson…***

CPSIA information can be obtained
at www.ICGtesting.com
Printed in the USA
BVHW060847051120
592523BV00012B/419